THE
GOD
WHO
HEARS

JAMES MERRITT

HARVEST HOUSE PUBLISHERS
EUGENE, OREGON

The author is represented by The Christopher Ferebee Agency, www.christopherferebee.com

Cover designed by Faceout Studio, Elisha Zepeda

Cover images © David M. Schrader / Shutterstock

Interior design by KUHN Design Group

Italics in Scripture verses is used for emphasis by the author.

For bulk, special sales, or ministry purchases, please call 1-800-547-8979.
Email: CustomerService@hhpbooks.com

This logo is a federally registered trademark of the Hawkins Children's LLC. Harvest House Publishers, Inc., is the exclusive licensee of this trademark.

The God Who Hears
Copyright © 2024 by James Merritt
Published by Harvest House Publishers
Eugene, Oregon 97408
www.harvesthousepublishers.com

ISBN 978-0-7369-8860-5 (Hardcover)
ISBN 978-0-7369-8861-2 (eBook)

Library of Congress Control Number: 2023940097

Printed in China

23 24 25 26 27 28 29 30 31 32 / RDS / 10 9 8 7 6 5 4 3 2 1

I dedicate this book to all the prayer warriors
I have pastored and connected with along so many avenues over the years
who have let me know of their constant prayers for me.

You know who you are.

CONTENTS

FOREWORD

GREG LAURIE

Have you ever been in what seemed like an impossible situation with no way out?

Have you ever had a desperate need that had no seemingly possible solution?

Have you ever thought there was no future for you, and that it was just too late?

If so, then you need to know more about the power of God and what can take place through prayer.

One thing that stands out in the pages of Scripture is that prayer can dramatically change situations, people, and, on occasion, even the course of nature itself. But what prayer changes the most is you and me.

God allows hardship and difficulties in our lives so He can reveal Himself and put His power and glory on display for those who are watching. When we pray, we're acknowledging our weakness and our need for God's help.

Maybe that's the reason we don't pray as much as we ought to. Prayer is an admission of weakness on our part, and some people don't like to admit they have a need.

The strongest man who ever lived was Jesus Christ, and we read repeatedly in the Gospels that Jesus prayed—and He prayed a lot. He would spend the night in prayer. He would rise up early while the disciples were still sleeping and pray. And as the crucifixion approached, He turned to the Father in prayer in the Garden of Gethsemane.

The Bible tells us that "while Jesus was here on earth, he offered prayers and pleadings, with a loud cry and tears, to the one who could rescue him from death. And God heard his prayers because of his deep reverence for God" (Hebrews 5:7 NLT). Notice the phrase "with a loud cry and tears." There's a place for that too in prayer.

So if Jesus, who is God, prayed a lot, then undoubtedly we need to pray a lot too.

God is deeply involved and deeply concerned about what you're facing right now. If it concerns you, then it concerns Him. But we also need to recognize that prayer is getting God's will on Earth, not our will in heaven.

As Christians, we know this, yet we would all have to admit that we don't pray as much as we ought. But I have good news for you…help is on the way!

My good friend Pastor James Merritt deals with how you can unlock your prayer life, and you are holding that book right now in your hand. He is one of the finest Bible teachers in the world today, and when he speaks or writes, I take the time to listen.

In *The God Who Hears*, Pastor James focuses on the prison prayers of the great apostle Paul and shares practical and applicable truth that will enhance your prayers.

Let's get started and learn more about prayer together!

YES, GOD HEARS US

If you believe in prayer at all, expect God to hear you.
If you do not expect, you will not have. God will not
hear you unless you believe He will hear you; but if you
believe He will, He will be as good as your faith.[1]

CHARLES SPURGEON

You hear prayers.

PSALM 65:2 NET

Here's a story you may have encountered before, but can you relate to it?
A young reporter in Israel was searching for a human-interest story when she learned about an old man who'd been praying at the Wailing Wall in the Old City of Jerusalem twice a day, every day, for many years. Sure enough, she found him there, standing as he rocked back and forth with eyes closed, beating his breast, raising his hands to God, passionately praying.

When he stopped, the reporter approached him and asked, "Sir, how many years have you been praying here?"

"Fifty," he told her.

"What do you pray for?"

"I pray for peace between the Jews and Arabs, for our children to grow up in safety and friendship. I especially pray for the peace of Jerusalem."

"Do you believe your prayers are effective?"

With apparent sadness, the old man replied, "Not really. I feel like I am talking to a wall."

Before you begin this devotional prayer journey, I believe I owe it to you to be upfront, candid, and transparent. Praying has always been hard work for me. Sometimes I've felt as though my prayers were just bouncing off the walls or the ceiling, never leaving the room, never moving the needle, and bringing frustration rather than exhilaration. I've even considered raising the white flag of surrender and giving up. So not only do I not think of myself as a great prayer warrior, but I'm still learning how to pray both effectively and with certainty that I'm truly connecting with God.

The truth is I'm not sure any Christian graduates from the school of prayer, so I'm guessing that you, too, would benefit from learning more about how to pray. Here's the first lesson we all need to learn, coming through what may be the three greatest words about prayer we'll ever hear:

God hears prayer

These simple, short, single-syllable words lined up in a sentence tell us why every follower of Jesus can pray not only consistently, constantly, and continuously, but also confidently. They can transform how we think about prayer, believing that our prayers can make an eternal difference in both our lives and the lives of others. But when I say God hears prayer, don't just take my word for it. Over and over in his Word, God himself tells us he hears when we call:

- The righteous cry out, and *the Lord hears* (Psalm 34:17).

- Before they call, I will answer; while they are still speaking, *I will hear* (Isaiah 65:24).

- Call to me and *I will answer you* (Jeremiah 33:3).

When you pray, you also have the Lord's full attention. He hangs on every word you say. He doesn't put you on hold, ask you to wait in line, or require you to make an appointment.

The second lesson we must learn was succinctly stated by English preacher Charles Spurgeon:

> *God will not hear you unless you believe he will hear you.*[2]

This makes sense, doesn't it? If you don't believe another person is listening during a conversation between the two of you, what will happen to your attempt to communicate? But again, his Word makes it clear that God *is* listening. First Peter 3:12 says, "The eyes of the Lord are on the righteous and his ears are attentive to their prayer."

Now, knowing and believing that God hears our prayers is foundational to our prayer lives, but we also need to know *how* to pray—to the glory of God but also because we want to make the connection with him we so crave. We want to replace the feeling we're not getting through to God with the knowledge that our prayers are truly soaring to his very throne room.

Here's a true story illustrating how important it is to make sure we're on heaven's wavelength—and that we know how to get there.

When Nelson Rockefeller was the vice president of the United States in the 1970s, he called one of his Secret Service agents, frustrated. He'd been calling the White House to speak to the president, but the operator kept hanging up on him even though he told her who he was. The agent discovered that, despite a special signal phone having been installed in his residence—a "drop line"—Rockefeller had been calling some number he looked up himself and using a regular phone. All he had to do was pick up the signal phone's receiver, and he'd be put right through.[3]

As you read about the apostle Paul's telling the churches in Ephesus, Philippi, and Colossae what and how he prayed for them, I believe you'll see that he had a direct "drop line" to God. After all, he knew he wasn't praying to just any god; he was praying to the God who hears, who listens. These prayers also serve as a divine model for how we can pray not just when we're in crisis but when we're not. In fact, the best way to learn how to pray when in a crisis is to pray when not in one.

Imprisoned when he wrote these letters we now call epistles, Paul shared prayers we can pray for others just as he did. But we can also personalize them and pray for ourselves. We can pray for anyone and anywhere, anytime, and under any circumstances.

Max Lucado said, "Our prayers may be awkward. Our attempts may be feeble. But since the power of prayer is in the One who hears it and not the one who says it, our prayers do make a difference."[4] I can assure you that as you learn from these prayers that are as much for us as they were for the churches to whom Paul wrote, your own prayers won't be awkward, your attempts won't be feeble, your petitions will make a difference, and you can rest assured they will be heard.

Let's begin this journey of learning how to pray to the God who hears.

EPHESIANS 1:15-23

Ever since I heard about your faith in the Lord Jesus and your love for all God's people, I have not stopped giving thanks for you, remembering you in my prayers. I keep asking that the God of our Lord Jesus Christ, the glorious Father, may give you the Spirit of wisdom and revelation, so that you may know him better. I pray that the eyes of your heart may be enlightened in order that you may know the hope to which he has called you, the riches of his glorious inheritance in his holy people, and his incomparably great power for us who believe. That power is the same as the mighty strength he exerted when he raised Christ from the dead and seated him at his right hand in the heavenly realms, far above all rule and authority, power and dominion, and every name that is invoked, not only in the present age but also in the one to come. And God placed all things under his feet and appointed him to be head over everything for the church, which is his body, the fullness of him who fills everything in every way.

NEVER GIVE UP ON GOD

When you feel like quitting, think about why you started.[1]

ANONYMOUS

For personal reasons, I can't disclose what I went through during the toughest two and a half years of my life, but I faced a situation I never dreamed I would. And after trying to fix it on my own, I finally realized the only thing I could do was pray. So I did, crying out to God over and over. But he didn't seem to be listening, and more than once I thought, *What's the use? Either God doesn't hear me, or I'm just not connecting with him.*

F.B. Meyer said, "The greatest tragedy of life is not unanswered prayer, but unoffered prayer."[2] Yet on one of the darkest, most depressing days of my whole ordeal, when I was about to give up on even asking God to help, this thought hit me: *If I give up on prayer, I give up on God.*

So as my trial persisted, I kept praying, day after day, asking for God's will to be done in my life and in this situation, no matter what the outcome would be.

Then literally all in one day, my prayer was answered in a far better way than I could have asked. And because of my experience in prayer throughout those two and a half years, I've come to understand the following two truths I believe are even more important than answered prayer:

1. *Prayer is almost never a one-and-done deal.* We aren't praying to a genie whose lamp we rub and then suddenly appears to grant whatever we wish. We're praying to the God who wants us to pray to him about any situation or concern not once but repeatedly, not only to practice the discipline of true prayer but to develop patience. To grow in our trust in him.

2. *Prayer is not for God to do something* for *us but to allow him to do something* in *us.* For so long I hadn't been ready for God to do what I wanted him to do *for* me because I wasn't hearing what he first wanted to do *in* me. We can't stop at hoping or even believing that God is listening; we have to listen to him too. William McGill nailed it when he said, "The value of persistent prayer is not that [God] will hear us, but that we will hear him."[3]

Not long after I entered this difficult period, someone I love and trust and knew what I was going through gave me a paperweight that still sits on my desk today. I saw it every time I sat down to spend time with God, and here are its three words as they appear:

Pray

Trust

Wait

There's no way around it. I wanted to pray. I understood trust. But the wait part? I wanted to pass. Yet powerful prayer is prevailing prayer. We pray.

We trust. We wait. And then we repeat all three. Giving up on prayer wasn't the way to go, because as I continued to pray, I grew more in tune with waiting for God's solution, believing it would come.

Hear this carefully: *The only failure in prayer is the failure to offer prayer.* Paul reminds us of the need for perseverance in prayer in his opening statement: "Ever since I heard about your faith in the Lord Jesus and your love for all God's people, I have not stopped giving thanks for you, remembering you in my prayers. I keep asking that the God of our Lord Jesus Christ, the glorious Father..." (Ephesians 1:15-16). Paul knew that when you give up on prayer, you give up on God. The oldest temptation in the book goes all the way back to the Garden of Eden when Satan tempted Adam and Eve to give up on God, and I don't have to tell you how disastrous that was!

Anyone who knows me understands I'm possibly the biggest Georgia Bulldogs fan on this planet, and I've discovered that, for me, being a devotee of the University of Georgia's football team relates to a biblical concept—no joke! Let me start by telling you the characteristics of a bulldog.

This dog will never win a beauty contest. Its nose is stuck up between its eyes, its legs are short and fat, and its shoulders are almost too wide for the rest of its body. But I discovered that the bulldog breed was developed during medieval times and was named because of its function. It gave the impression of being "a little bull," and so the dogs were originally used to attack bulls in an arena to stir them up for combat.

I went on to learn that the very physical characteristics that make this dog somewhat ugly are what make it powerful. Its shoulders help it stand its ground during combat. Its nose is placed in an upward position so that when another animal attacks, it can hold on to it and breathe at the same time. Furthermore, its opponent can't block the flow of oxygen to force the dog to let it go, and the bulldog has such tenacity that it won't let go until its attacker is incapacitated or dead!

When as an old man Joshua was saying farewell to the Israelite leaders, he told them, "Hold fast to the Lord your God, as you have until now" (Joshua 23:8). I've learned that when it comes to prayer, I need to hold on to God and his promises with bulldog tenacity![4] Don't let go of your hope in God nor of the God of hope. No matter what problem you need solved, what question you need answered, or from what difficulty you need deliverance, keep praying to the God who will never fail you.

Father, I will never give up on prayer, for I will never give up on you! When all else around me is falling apart, coming unhinged, and vanishing beneath my feet, I will tie the rope of prayer around your feet and hold to your unchanging power and presence that always comes with and through prayer to the one who always keeps his promises. In the name of the One who taught us to pray and never give up, amen.

LOOK OUT AS YOU LOOK UP

*Your prayer for someone may or may not change
them, but it always changes you.*[1]
CRAIG GROESCHEL

don't want to be super spiritual, nor do I want to pretend I never think about myself first when I'm in trouble, so I'll confess how *I* would pray if I, like Paul, were in prison for following God's call on my life. Short, sweet, and straight to the point, these six words ought to do it: *God, get me out of here!* I would pray for acquittal, a reprieve, or even a Special Forces rescue—whatever it would take to regain my freedom.

Yet, amazingly, as we look at more of this first of Paul's prison prayers, we see that he didn't pray for deliverance. He didn't pray for himself at all. He prayed for others, for the church in Ephesus.

Read again how this passage begins and then goes on, noticing two words repeated over and over—*you* and *your*:

Ever since I heard about your faith in the Lord Jesus and your love for all God's people, I have not stopped giving thanks for you, remembering you in my prayers. I keep asking that the God of our Lord Jesus Christ, the glorious Father, may give you the Spirit of wisdom and revelation, so that you may know him better. I pray that the eyes of your heart may be enlightened in order that you may know the hope to which he has called you, the riches of his glorious inheritance in his holy people (Ephesians 1:15-18).

Paul wasn't looking in a mirror as he prayed; he was looking "out a window." He was looking out as he was looking up, his first instinct to pray for others.

Honestly, that seems not only counterintuitive but counterproductive. After all, who needed God's help for himself more than this man who didn't even know if he'd live another day? But upon both closer inspection and further reflection, we see there was a method to Paul's madness. His upward focus led to an outward focus, to a heart for others in his prayer life.

So many of our opening prayer requests can be categorized under three groups of three words:

Please give me. We pray for God's provision—for a job, transportation, funding, or anything else we need.

Please heal me. We pray for our own sickness, whether physical, emotional, mental, or anything else that qualifies as an illness of some sort.

Please help me. We need to pass that test, do well in that interview, or stay safe as we travel.

There's nothing wrong with those prayers, yet a heart for God leads first to prayer for other people, asking him to intervene and care for them before asking him to intervene and care for us. The heart for God is not me-centered but others-centered.

Consider what many believe is the greatest verse in the Bible: "God so loved the world that he gave his one and only Son, that whoever believes in him shall not perish but have eternal life" (John 3:16). God sent Jesus so that he might do his work of salvation in us. He didn't send him to change our environment, change our circumstances, change our financial position, or change our standing in society. He sent him so *we* could change, made possible because in his great love, God chose to focus on us.

Let's make this practical because one of the best lessons I've learned in my own prayer life is that when my upward look leads me to an outward look, it changes my inward look. When I pray for others, my prayer changes me.

Has someone really hurt you, perhaps not physically but emotionally? This has happened to me more than once, and just like you probably did if it happened to you, I immediately battled bitterness. I so badly wanted to claim this Irish saying:

> May those who love us love us.
> And for those who don't love us, may God turn their hearts.
> And if he cannot turn their hearts, may he turn their ankles,
> so we may know them by their limping.[2]

One of the hardest things you will ever do is to pray for those who hurt you—even your enemies. But Jesus knew what he was doing when he told his listeners, "You have heard that it was said, 'Love your neighbor and hate your enemy.' But I tell you, love your enemies and pray for those who persecute you, that you may be children of your Father in heaven" (Matthew 5:43-45).

You see, there's no greater way to love others than to pray for them, and it's extremely difficult if not impossible to stay bitter toward anyone we pray for. When we pray for the sick and suffering, we're reminded to be grateful for our own health. When we pray for those being persecuted, we're moved to be grateful for the protection we all too often take for granted. And when we pray for those who hurt us, true forgiveness becomes all the more possible in our hearts. Prayer forces bitterness out and forgiveness in—that's just the way it works. When we pray for others, God does a work in us.

Here are a few quotes focusing on intercession—prayer on behalf of others' needs:

- If we truly love people, we will desire for them far more than it is within our power to give them, and this will lead us to prayer: Intercession is a way of loving others. —Richard J. Foster

- No man can do me a truer kindness in this world than to pray for me. —Charles Spurgeon

- We are never more like Christ than in prayers of intercession. —Austin Phelps[3]

I believe all that is true. So when you pray to the God who hears, look out as you look up, and you'll find him doing his greatest work in you.

Father, may my prayers be first upward focused, then outward focused, and only then inward focused. It's as simple as that. Amen.

DO YOU KNOW WHO YOU ARE TALKING TO?

Once you become aware that the main business that you are here for is to know God, most of life's problems fall into place of their own accord.[1]

J.I. PACKER

We can't know God—and we certainly can't know him better—unless we're connecting with him. Here's a story that illustrates this point: Just before World War II, a school fire broke out in Itasca, Texas, killing 263 children and leaving the town with no school building all throughout the war. When the townspeople were finally able to construct a new one, they installed what was called "the finest sprinkler system in the world." This feature granted them a powerful source they could depend on after such a tragedy.

Or so they thought. While adding a wing to the school seven years later, workers made an astonishing discovery: This amazing sprinkler system had never been connected.[2] All those years, the people never realized their prized system lacked the most necessary component for it to work.

As we continue to dive into Paul's first prison prayer, we learn how to truly connect with the God who hears. In Ephesians 1:17, he tells the church in Ephesus what he consistently requests of the Lord on their behalf—and why: "I keep asking that the God of our Lord Jesus Christ, the glorious Father, may give you the Spirit of wisdom and revelation, so that you may know him better." The apostle asks not for what the Ephesians most want, whatever that might be, but for what they most need—to know God better.

To be clear, the word *know* in this verse doesn't mean a casual acquaintance with someone. Many of the people I say I know I've merely been introduced to or I know their name or face, but I don't really know them. The Greek word for "know" here and in other parts of Scripture refers to an "intimate knowledge." Not just a philosophical, intellectual, or even emotional knowledge of God but a personal, experiential, transformational knowledge of God.[3]

Before we explore why his asking for the Spirit of wisdom and revelation for the Ephesians was uppermost in Paul's mind, think about how and why knowing God is the bull's-eye of the Christian life. We are to obey God, but we won't obey him until we trust him, and we won't trust him until we know him. And so the better we know God, the more we'll trust him, and the more we trust him, the more we'll obey him.

Growing as a Christian begins with knowing God, but we can't just know of God or about him and expect to grow. That's knowledge, not wisdom. Knowledge is knowing a tomato is a fruit, but wisdom is not putting tomato in a fruit salad. With knowledge we can see how God has revealed himself, but through wisdom we can know the God who has revealed himself.

Jesus said to his Father, "This is eternal life: that they know you, the only true God" (John 17:3). In a commentary, Doug McIntosh wrote, "To know God and to find one's full satisfaction in that knowledge is the ultimate goal of Christian experience. The Lord's greatest delight comes when His people discover the ultimate value lies in the knowledge of God."[4]

But if we don't truly know God, our prayers might seem as if they aren't connecting. The Welsh preacher D. Martyn Lloyd-Jones said that ensuring we know the God we're praying to is the key to the whole question of prayer, and I agree.[5]

Of all the books I've read, few impacted my life like *Knowing God*, written by J.I. Packer. In it, he asked this series of questions and made these statements: "What were we made for? To know God. To what aim should we set ourselves? To know God. What is the 'eternal life' that Jesus gives? Knowledge of God."[6]

Now let's go back to what Paul conveys we need to do first thing in order to know God: ask the Lord to give us "the Spirit of wisdom and revelation." We need that help because we can't gain true wisdom on our own. In the Bible, God tells us who he is, including the One from whom all things come, and he shows us who he is through his Son, Jesus. That's knowledge granted us through God's revelation.

But with wisdom—gained through prayer—we can better know the God who has revealed himself. After all, those we know best are the people we spend the most time with. This is why knowing God better is the primary reason to pray, and the sweetest result when we do pray is knowing God better.

By the way, you can ask for the Spirit of wisdom and revelation on behalf of both believers and unbelievers. What should we ask for an unbeliever? That they will know God. What should we ask for believers? That they will know God better.

The late great pastor of the Tenth Presbyterian Church in Philadelphia, James Montgomery Boice, was in a question and answer session for the meeting of the postcollege group in his church. They asked him this question: "Dr. Boice, what do you think is the greatest lack among evangelical Christians in America today?" This was quite a few years ago, and Dr. Boice said it was the first time he had been asked that question, but I believe the answer that he gave is just as accurate today as it was then. He said, unequivocally, "I think that the greatest need of the evangelical church today is for professing Christians really to know God."[7]

There's no better way for us to begin any prayer than to ask God to grant us the Spirit of wisdom and revelation so that we might know him better and truly connect with him. Paul understood knowing God to be a matter of prayer and prayer to be a matter of knowing God, and so must we. When you pray, make sure you know who you are talking to.

Father, through your Holy Spirit this very minute, give me the Spirit of wisdom and revelation that I might know you better. I am so joyful to be talking with the God who now and forevermore is good, gracious, glorious, knowable, and hears me when I pray. In the name of Jesus, amen.

4

OPEN THE EYES
OF MY HEART, LORD

*Better to be blind and see with your heart
than to have two good eyes and see nothing.*[1]

HELEN KELLER

What you're doing right now is nothing short of a miracle. You may be thinking, *Just reading your book?* Well, for me that *is* a miracle! But unless you're reading with braille, the reason you can read is that you have wonder-working, miraculous machines called eyes.

What eyes can do is among the most incredible phenomena in the universe. Yet even though they are responsible for 90 percent of all the information we learn, through observation, we take them for granted every day. The muscles in our eyes are even the most active muscles in our entire bodies.[2]

Here are just some facts about your eyes you ought to consider:

- Eyes are the second most complex part of your body—only being surpassed in complexity by the brain.

- Only 1/6 of the eye is exposed to the human world.

- A fingerprint contains 40 unique traits, but your eyes contain 256, which is why retina security scans are more secure.

- Eyes manage 80 percent of all the information you will ever take in in your lifetime.

- An eye has more than 2 million working parts.[3]

In their book *In His Image*, Dr. Paul Brand and Philip Yancey tell us,

> Our brains do not receive photographic images of anything. Rather, some of the 127,000,000 rods and cones get "excited" by light waves and fire off messages into the 1,000,000 fibers of the optic nerve, which coils like a thick television cable back into the recesses of the brain. Impulses from the retina race along the fibers of the optic nerve, fan out in the brain, and finally slam into the visual cortex, stimulating the miracle of sight.[4]

Why am I talking about eyes in a book about prayer? Because if we understand how incredible seeing with our eyes is—made possible by our heavenly creator of our bodies—perhaps we can understand how even more incredible it is to see with the eyes of our hearts. On behalf of the church in Ephesus, Paul prays "that the eyes of your heart may be enlightened in order that you may know the hope to which [God] has called you" (Ephesians 1:18).

We wear glasses or contact lenses to enhance our physical vision, but biblically speaking, our hearts represent our will, our mind, our emotions, and our desires. We need to continually ask God to enhance our spiritual vision so with our whole being we can know the hope that comes from only him.

The Greek word for "enlightened" is *phos*, which means "light," and the word for "know" literally means "to see." So Paul is saying he believes prayer, which comes from the heart, should be an eye-opening experience. As we pray, then, we are to ask God to help us see—to know—the hope to which he's called us. Think of it this way: We are to pray that we might see the hope we have in God and to know the God who gives us hope.

Understand, hope is not wishful thinking. I plan to play golf tomorrow, and I hope it won't rain. And when I first met my wife, Teresa, I hoped she would go out with me. Many high school seniors hope they will get into their dream college. But that isn't what God's Word means by hope. Hope is the absolute, irrevocable, unshakeable confidence that God will do what he's promised to do.

Let's look at how God's hope has to do with not just our present but with our past and future as well, how his hope makes the difference throughout our very existence:

> *Hope for our past:* When the eyes of our hearts are enlightened, we see the hope of our salvation, the certainty that in Jesus our sins have been totally and finally forgiven. This is the hope that takes care of our past.

> *Hope for our present:* When the eyes of our hearts are enlightened, we see the hope that God will give us the power through his Spirit to live pure and holy, to give us the wisdom to know his will as he reveals it, and then the strength to do it. That takes care of our present.

> *Hope for our future:* Finally, when the eyes of our hearts are enlightened, we see the hope that one day we will be with the Lord in heaven and will be just like him with a new and resurrected body. This hope takes care of our future.

We also need to see God himself with our hearts. A little girl was on a cruise with her dad, sailing around Catalina Island off the coast of Southern California. It was one of those beautiful, clear days when it seems like you can see forever. She looked at her father with a big smile on her face and said, "Daddy, I can look farther than my eyes can see." God wants you to see him in all his glory with the eyes of your heart.

In the nineteenth century, Clara H. Scott wrote these lyrics to the hymn "Open My Eyes, That I May See." She wasn't writing about the eyes in our heads but eyes of our heart. The first stanza reads,

> Open my eyes that I may see
> glimpses of truth thou hast for me;
> Place in my hands the wonderful key
> that shall unclasp and set me free.
> Silently now I wait for thee,
> ready, my God, thy will to see.
> Open my eyes, illumine me,
> Spirit divine![5]

If you're convinced a situation you're in is hopeless, please know it's not. As long as there's a God who's listening—and that's both now and forever—there's hope that can set you free from worry. The God who's already taken care of your past and has already promised to take care of your future will certainly take care of your present. You can't see that with the eyes in your head, but you can ask the Lord to help you see it with the eyes of your heart. And, oh, what a sight you will see!

Open the eyes of my heart, Lord, that I might see the hope to which you have called me—that my past is forgiven, my future is secure, and my present is safe in your hands. In the name of the Lord who's the source of all hope, amen.

5

THE GREATEST
INHERITANCE

Your worth is what you are worth to God.
Jesus died for you. You are of infinite value.[1]

NICKY GUMBEL

When I was pastoring my first church full-time out of seminary, we held what we called a Starlight Crusade in a stadium. We brought in celebrities, well-known sports figures, and others to draw a crowd, and then I preached the gospel.

On one occasion I'd invited evangelist Rick Stanley, Elvis Presley's stepbrother—who died a few years ago—to be my guest. Elvis had already passed away, and while Rick and I were seated side by side on the platform, I leaned over and asked him what I meant to be an innocent question: "How much did Elvis leave when he died?"

He immediately snapped, "He left it all!"

One day we're all going to "leave it all," and we're told one generation will leave more than any before it. A 2019 *Forbes* article said, "Baby Boomers, the generation of people born between 1944 and 1964, are expected to transfer $30 trillion in wealth to younger generations over the next many years. This jaw-dropping amount has led many journalists and financial experts to refer to the gradual event as the "great wealth transfer."[2]

But inheritance isn't just about monetary wealth, especially in God's Word. Paul asked the Lord to give the Ephesians the Spirit of wisdom and revelation so they might know him better, that the eyes of their hearts would be enlightened so they would know the hope to which God had called them. But then he said he'd been praying for them to know something else: "the riches of his glorious inheritance in his holy people" (Ephesians 1:18).

When you hear the word "inheritance" for Christians, you most likely think of what we'll inherit as part of God's family. In other words, what's waiting for us once we get to heaven. And understanding the value of that inheritance is crucial. Philip Henry was a seventeenth-century clergyman, and his future wife, a Miss Matthews, certainly did:

> A traditional story illustrates her temperament when barriers were being placed in the way of their forthcoming marriage. Among other objections urged by her friends against the connection was this—that, although Mr. Henry was a gentleman, and a scholar, and an excellent preacher, he was quite a stranger, and they did not even know where he came from. "True," replied Miss Matthews, "but I know where he is going, and I should like to go with him."[3]

A glorious inheritance is awaiting every child of God, an inheritance so great that we're told that our eye has not seen, nor has our ear heard, nor can the human mind conceive how great our inheritance really is (1 Corinthians 2:9). Paul refers to this inheritance back up in verse 14, when speaking of the Holy Spirit, "who is a deposit *guaranteeing our inheritance*." The word used here for "inheritance" is the same word used in verse 18, except here it's used as the "believers' inheritance," our share in heaven.[4]

The only difference between our inheritance of heaven from ones like a generational transfer of wealth is that we're not waiting for our Father to die to receive it. He's waiting for us to die to give it!

But there's another inheritance as well, one that tells us just how valuable God's people—all of us who are his children—are to him. This is not the inheritance we are going to get from God. It is about God's inheritance he is going to gain in us! Let's read this part of Ephesians 1:18 again: "the riches of his glorious inheritance in his holy people."

You'd better sit down if you're standing.

God has an inheritance as well, and all his children—including *you*—are that inheritance! His inheritance is not the galaxies, the solar systems, the planets, the universe, and everything in it. He already owns all that. His inheritance is in his holy people—us. We are what he's waiting for. We are his treasure. We are his riches.

The book of Ephesians isn't the first place in the Bible God's people are called his inheritance. In Deuteronomy 4:20, the Israelites were told, "The LORD took you and brought you out of the iron-smelting furnace, out of Egypt, *to be the people of his inheritance, as you now are*."

Today, the world may look at Jesus' followers—his body, the church—and think we're not much to look at. Some think we're even worthy of persecution in one form or another. But God says we're so valuable to him that we're his inheritance. When we give all of ourselves to Jesus, he gives all of himself to us. We get him, but he gets us too, and he considers us his riches.

Now, you might be thinking, *Riches? Seems like the Lord got the worst end of that deal*. Well, that reminds me of a story that, though fiction, makes my next point. During a fierce argument, a husband said to his wife, "Men have better judgment than women."

Angry, she responded with, "That's true. Just look at us. You wisely married me, but I unwisely married you!"

The God who hears doesn't see us that way. As his redeemed children, we are his prized possessions. And if you have a heart for God, deep down you can't wait to be with him in heaven, just as I believe he's eager to receive you.

Father, help me realize just how valuable I am to you. Help me remember my value doesn't lie in my ability, intellect, wealth, or personality. My value lies in your love for me and what you've done to make sure you inherit me. In Jesus' name I pray, amen.

6

POWER UP

I have learned there is nothing too great for God's power to deal with.[1]
JOSH MCDOWELL

f it's to be, it's up to me is a mantra repeated in our culture over and over in one form or another. Have you heard of it? Have you even said it or at least thought it? In some cases, expending all that solo effort works, but when it comes to living the Christian life—to getting through our adversities and coming out victorious—we don't have the power to make that happen within ourselves. This is why Paul prayed for the Ephesians to know God's "incomparably great power for us who believe" (Ephesians 1:19).

If you study Ephesians 1:19 in the original Greek, you really begin to appreciate what Paul is doing here. He's throwing even the kitchen sink at the church, trying to explain just how great God's power truly is. The word "incomparably" means "to surpass" or "to exceed."[2] And the word for "great" is the Greek word *megethos*, from which we get the word *megaton* that describes the power of an atomic bomb—an "explosive force equivalent to that of one million tons of TNT."[3] This is the only place the word *megethos* is found in the entire New Testament.[4]

Then to emphasize just how great this power is, in verse 20 Paul goes on to say, "That power is the same as the mighty strength [God] exerted when he raised Christ from the dead." Though the word "power" is repeated, this is a different Greek word that gives us the English word "energy." The word "mighty" is from the Greek word *kratos*, which means "might" or "ruling power."[5] (A democracy is where the people rule, an aristocracy is where the wealthy rule, but the entire universe is a theocracy because everything is under God's rule.)

All this is important because when we add it up, we see that we should pray, *God, today in everything I do, help me know your incomparably great power according to the power of the power of your power!* That's a pretty powerful statement! Normally you would never ask someone to tell you how powerful they are, but God invites us to ask him about his power and to know it.

Now, it's one thing to know the God of power, but we should also know the power of God. It's one thing to believe that God is all-powerful, but it's another to know that power, experience that power, and believe that power lives in us. In other words, it's incredible to know we have access to all the power we need to do what we ought to do and to be what we ought to be— all that we cannot do in our own power.

We also need to know the power of God to understand what we need to understand. Jesus said to Sadducees, who believed there was no resurrection, "You are in error because you do not know the Scriptures *or the power of God*" (Matthew 22:29). Psalm 147:5 says, "Great is our Lord and mighty in power."

Knowing and truly experiencing God's power comes through prayer to the God who hears. How many times have we failed where we might have succeeded because we counted on *our* power rather than on counting on *God's* power? How many times have we tried to make it on our own rather than asking God for his power? Oswald Chambers said, "Every element of our own self-reliance must be put to death by the power of God."[6]

Have you ever considered just how remarkable God's power is? Let's go back to the atomic bomb. In 1942, Italian and later naturalized American physicist Enrico Fermi unleashed the power of the atom by splitting it through a process called nuclear fission. And then the people of the world discovered how powerful that power is when on August 6, 1945, the first atomic bomb was dropped over Hiroshima, Japan. When it exploded, it

> reached a temperature of several million degrees Celsius, the temperature of the core of the sun. When the bomb exploded at 8:16:02 local time, four square miles of the city were instantly and completely devastated...The bomb produced so much energy that the glare of the blast would have been visible from Jupiter, roughly 390 million miles away...The energy produced by that bomb was the by-product of a subatomic reaction that used only 1 percent of two pounds of uranium. One-third of one ounce of uranium was translated into an explosion two thousand times more powerful than that of any bomb in the history of warfare up to that time.[7]

Now, if there's that much energy in one-third of one ounce of uranium, how much power do you think the creator of the atom has at his disposal and is at the disposal of those of us who believe?

Whatever you're facing today, as a believer you have within you the power of the very God who created everything. Knowing that no matter what gets you down, you can power up and power through with the power God grants those who believe should give you the boldness, confidence, and peace you need.

This is jumping ahead a little, but in Ephesians 3:20-21, Paul concludes another message to the Ephesians with "according to his power that is at work within us, to him be glory." Amen!

All-powerful God, I know your incomparably great power is always available to me, for I believe in you. I trust you to give me the power I need to do what I need to do and to be what I need to be for your glory. In Jesus' name, amen.

STRONGER
THAN YOU THINK

You are stronger than you think,
because the power of Almighty God is available to you.
Your strength is renewed when you trust in Him.[1]

KENDRA TILLMAN

L et's talk more about God's power, because Paul really calls our attention
to it when he writes that it is "the same as the mighty strength he exerted
when he raised Christ from the dead" (Ephesians 1:19-20).

If someone asked you how physically strong you are, you *could* respond
only verbally. For example, you might claim the ability to bench your weight
and then leave it at that. But to *prove* you can do it, you'd have to actually
bench your weight where that person can see you do it.

People who have performed the greatest feats of strength ever recorded
were indeed strong, but, of course, they proved it. Here are just four histor-
ical feats of strength that make my point:

- William Bankier—As part of his act, Bankier would harness-lift an elephant. He could also jump over the back of a chair, frontward or backward, while holding a 56-pound weight in each hand. Another celebrated routine, the 'Tomb of Hercules,' saw the strongman support a piano with a six-person orchestra and a dancer.

- Donald Dinnie—His most legendary effort remains a challenge to strongmen today: The legendary 'Dinnie Stones' are two granite boulders weighing a combined 733 pounds, which Dinnie in 1860 carried for more than 17 feet across the width of the Potarch Bridge.

- Thomas Topham—In 1741, Topham lifted three barrels weighing 1,336 pounds, to commemorate Admiral Vernon's taking of Portobello, which led to England's takeover of Panama.

- Paul Anderson—A September 1957 guest spot on *The Ed Sullivan Show* saw him lift a crowd of celebrities on a platform, among them boxer Jack Dempsey. He could drive a 20-penny nail through two wooden boards using only his thumb and lift two 85-pound dumbbells with his little finger. He is among the strongest humans to ever walk the planet, with official numbers at 440 pounds for a clean and jerk, 930 pounds for a back squat, and a 6,270-pound backlift.[2]

Impressed? Humanly speaking, we should all be impressed. But these feats of strength and all others combined pale in comparison to the strength God has just on the tip of one of his fingers. And we know this is true because he shows us it's true.

You don't have to look very far in this world to see God's impressive power. The first verse of the Bible, "In the beginning God created the heavens and the earth" (Genesis 1:1), never ceases to amaze me. To think that the Lord just spoke and the sun began to shine, the moon began to glow, the stars began to twinkle, the planets began to spin, and the galaxies expanded where once there was nothing is astounding—unless we acknowledge how powerful God truly is. Through his creation, it's easy to see his divine and unparalleled muscles flex.

Yet how does God's feat of creation compare to Jesus' resurrection? Just think about what's at stake. If Jesus' body were rotting somewhere in a Middle Eastern grave, what he taught would be irrelevant. How he lived would be meaningless. Who he really was would be at best debatable. But he was indeed supernaturally raised from the dead, and not only does this prove that he was and is God, but it was also the greatest display of power the world has ever been given. God's power.

Consider any kind of power you want—financial, intellectual, nuclear, atomic—and the one thing that power can't do is bring a dead man back to life. And not only that, but to do so with a body that can never die again. When considering what the odds are that Jesus' resurrection from the dead actually happened, many people would say zero. And I agree that the odds are absolutely impossible—*apart from the power of an omnipotent God.*

The odds of making a hole-in-one is 1 in 12,500. The odds of becoming president of the United States is 1 in 10,000,000. The odds of winning the lottery is 1 in 259,000,000. The odds of winning the lottery after surviving a lightning strike is 1 in 2.6 trillion.[3] But because of an empty tomb, we know the odds for Jesus' resurrection were 100 percent. By God's power, he was raised from the dead.

One of the reasons our prayers can seem powerless is that we greatly underestimate God's power. And maybe that's why, when writing to the Ephesian church, Paul called attention to the strength of God's power by citing his strength in the resurrection. I think he not only wanted them to know the incredible power of God, but also the incredible power prayer ignites. God's resurrection power is activated when we pray, and that power should motivate us to pray even more.

When we need God's strength—and when do we not?—1 Chronicles 16:11 advises us well: "Look to the LORD." With prayer, you really are stronger than you think, not because of what you can do, but because of what God has done.

When you celebrate Easter and the empty tomb pops into your mind, remember that with God's power, the power of the God who hears, you can have the strength to overcome anything. The author of Psalm 73 wrote, "My flesh and my heart may fail, but God is the strength of my heart and my portion forever" (verse 26). And Ephesians 6:10 says, "Be strong in the Lord and in his mighty power."

God, I often feel weak, powerless, and helpless, but I believe that the power you exerted when you raised your Son from the dead is available to me, giving me the strength to be victorious in every circumstance I face, confidence in every problem I need to solve, and assurance in every question I need to have answered. Truthfully, because of you, I am stronger than I think. Amen.

SIT NEXT TO ME

*Sitting silently at the feet of Jesus is of more worth
than all the clatter of Martha's dishes.*[1]

CHARLES SPURGEON

t's not every day that you get to eat a meal sitting with a former president of the United States, but years ago my two oldest sons, James and Jonathan, and I had that privilege. We'd been invited to a lunch by a man who through some God-ordained circumstances had become a good friend. He was running for governor in Georgia, and I was asked to speak on his behalf. President George H. W. Bush, who had just left office, was there as well.

To my great surprise, the three of us, along with the candidate, were seated at a table with the president. My sons and I were in awe as we talked to a man who had once been the most powerful person on earth and still probably had more influence than most other Americans except the current US president.

President Bush graciously said we could ask him about anything on any topic, and that raised the level of our excitement and enthusiasm even more. The entire experience soared to a different height altogether. I wish I'd had a way to record that conversation, and I wish I remembered more of what was said. But I do remember wishing our time with this gracious man would never end.

We've been reminded that we pray to a God whose power is unlimited—the power that was manifested at the empty tomb when he raised Christ from the dead. We pray to the risen Lord! But Jesus' resurrection was only the beginning. Paul tells the Ephesians that God "seated [Christ] at his right hand in the heavenly realms" (Ephesians 1:20). When did this take place? At Jesus' ascension.

Much thought has been given to the incarnation of Jesus and his resurrection, but when it comes to prayer, we should give more thought to his ascension. Why? Because it's the ascended Lord who prays for us while we're praying to him.

Understand that the ascension is not simply Jesus leaving Earth and returning to heaven. It wasn't just a change in altitude or location for him. In his book *Encounters with Jesus*, the late pastor and author Tim Keller wrote that Jesus' ascension was more like a coronation. When someone is crowned a king or queen, an elaborate ceremony takes place and they "ascend to the throne." Once seated on that throne, they have a new relationship with others, along with "new powers and privileges to exercise authority."[2]

In the incarnation, Jesus became the God-man fully divine yet fully human, and as Keller goes on to say, "At the ascension Jesus leaves the space-time continuum and passes into the presence of the Father."[3] After his ascension, Christ was completely glorified and not limited by time or space.

He also began interceding for us at the right hand of the Father (Hebrews 7:25). The apostle Peter said Jesus is the One "who has gone into heaven and is at God's right hand—with angels, authorities and powers in submission to him" (1 Peter 3:22). "Right hand" is "a place of honor."[4] When we stand before God, we will bow at his feet in worship, but Jesus sits in a place of honor at his right hand. As Harold W. Hoehner said, that's where every spiritual benefit we have comes from.[5]

Can you just imagine the unbelievable celebration that took place when God's Son returned to heaven? Perhaps the greatest sermon I've ever heard was preached by Dr. Jerry Vines. Titled "Our Ascended Lord," it was magisterial in the beautiful and imaginative way he painted a picture of the Lord's returning to heaven. He described Jesus walking through the streets of gold lined with angels on both sides and said he could just imagine hearing them shout out welcomes like these:

"Jesus, we sure have missed you!"

"Lord, we're so glad you're back!"

"Jesus, it just hasn't been heaven without you!"[6]

What a scene that must have been!

And not only is the risen Son of God seated on the throne of heaven at the right hand of the Father, but God has seated us with him. Paul tells us this in Ephesians 2:6: "God raised us up with Christ and seated us with him in the heavenly realms." Every time you pray, then, the Lord Jesus is saying to you, *Be sure you're sitting here—right next to me.*

When Martha was distracted by preparing a meal in the kitchen while her sister, Mary, sat at Jesus' feet to learn from him, he invited her to sit with him as well. He told her what he might tell us today: "Few things are needed—or indeed only one" (Luke 10:42). Not only must we spend time with Jesus undistracted, but we are to sit with him. We're invited to put the worries and challenges of this world aside and be with our Lord and Savior.

How can we ever doubt that God hears our prayers; is attentive to our prayers; and is willing, ready, and able to answer our prayers according to his will when Jesus is sitting at God's right hand and expects us to sit with him? Just that thought alone leads me to pray right now!

Precious Lord, I accept your invitation to come sit next to you, pour out my heart to you, and speak to you as you speak for me to my heavenly Father. I thank you that the door is always open and the seat is always available. So right now I'll sit with you a while. Amen.

THE ULTIMATE AUTHORITY

Prayer is the risen Jesus coming in with His resurrection power...
using his authority to enter any situation and change things.[1]

OLE HALLESBY

As Bob Buford wrote in his book *Halftime*, there's no such thing as a life without authority.[2] The moment we take our first breath, we're under authority whether or not we realize it. Take the authority of physical laws, for example. We don't have to learn to be under the authority of gravity. We figure out it's a given the first time we misstep and fall flat on our face. In essence, Buford says, "You can choose the game, but you can't choose the rules."[3]

Sports games give us great examples of this, as Buford goes on to explain: "If you're going to play tennis, you have to serve behind the line and keep the ball within the sidelines. If your sport is basketball, you must dribble the ball up the court instead of running with it...Follow the rules, and your chances of winning are greater."[4] What's true about a game is even more true of God. Not only does all authority come from him, but he's the ultimate authority. And we can't win in this life unless we know and accept that fact.

When a culture increasingly rejects the very principle of authority, that's a sign it's also rejecting God and headed for trouble. The philosopher Charles Taylor wrote about how the West changed from a culture of "authority" to a culture of "authenticity." What he meant is that at one time our culture lived by *external* authority structures (God, the Bible, tradition, social mores, consensus, and so on) that told us what we should do. But there's been a tectonic shift. Now many people in the West live according to what their *internal* structure (their "authentic self") wants them to do.[5]

It's exactly this kind of individualistic, rebellious thinking that drives much of atheism, agnosticism, and humanism. The atheist philosopher Thomas Nagel was being honest when he said, "It isn't just that I don't believe in God and, naturally, hope that I am right in my belief. It's that I hope there is no God! I don't want there to be a God; I don't want the universe to be like that… this cosmic authority problem is not a rare condition."[6]

But religion philosopher Paul Mosher said, "It would be a strange, defective God who didn't pose a serious cosmic authority problem for humans. Part of the status of being *God*, after all, is that God has a unique authority, or lordship, over humans. Since we humans aren't God, the true God would have authority over us and would seek to correct our profoundly selfish ways.[7]

The shift away from God's authority illustrates why what Paul says next in Ephesians 1 is not only crucial to understanding what prayer is all about, but also to understanding the Lord to whom we pray. He says that, seated next to his Father, Christ is "far above all rule and authority, power and dominion" (Ephesians 1:21).

Paul is making the point that when we pray, we're praying to the ultimate authority. This is some of the strongest rhetoric we find about the authority of Jesus anywhere in the Bible. Everything and everyone everywhere are under his feet. Satan and his demons, Gabriel and his angels, a British king, a Chinese dictator, an American president, a four-star general, and you and

I are all under his authority. So when we pray to Christ, we truly are praying to the only being in the universe who has all authority over any other authority and is in fact the source of all other authority.

Consider when Jesus himself declared his authority, one of the greatest assertions in his entire ministry: "All authority in heaven and on earth has been given to me" (Matthew 28:18). In his book *Surprised by Jesus*, Tim Stafford wrote,

> If he had said, "All authority in Jerusalem has been given to me," it would have been an extraordinary claim. The chief priest or Pilate or any of the Roman centurions had a different idea about who held authority in Jerusalem. Yet Jesus claimed more than Jerusalem. He claimed authority in heaven and on earth. He proclaimed himself bigger than Augustus Caesar. He claimed to be the Messiah.[8]

Another reason, then, we should pray constantly, consistently, and confidently is that we're praying to the One who has ultimate authority over every foe we fight and every fear we face.

There is no greater example of our submission to that authority than when we pray acknowledging that we have neither the power nor the authority to do all we need to do and to be all we need to be. But we can go to the One who does, the God who not only hears us but enables us. Proverbs 3:6 says if you submit to him, God will "make your paths straight." And Luke 1:37 says, "No word from God will ever fail."

No believer should live a discouraged, defeated life. We can always go to the One who is the ultimate authority and can enable us to overcome every foe, every fear, and every failure.

Lord, I'm so thankful that when I feel as though I'm at the end of my rope, only you have true authority over me because you are the ultimate authority. Today I will live my life under your authority, knowing that because I love you, you will exercise it to work all things together for my good. In Jesus' name I pray, amen.

10

IT'S HIS CHURCH

We do not want a church that will move with the world.
We want a church that will move the world.[1]

G.K. Chesterton

By the very nature of my vocation as a pastor, I work at the church, in the church, and for the church. The church is not my life, but it's undeniably been a huge part of it ever since I was born. And to put it in business terms, because of both my personal involvement in and financial commitment to the church, both universally and locally, you might say I'm one of its major stockholders.

Now, the truth is if you're a follower of Jesus, you certainly have stock in the universal church, and hopefully you're committed to, attend, serve, and financially support your local church, which makes you a stockholder there too. But I have to admit a sober reality about the church of today to my fellow stockholder.

If the church was a publicly traded corporation, I fear the *Wall Street Journal* would not be too flattering about our prospects. Stock prices have been plummeting for a long time, and more people than ever have not only sold their stock but are so dissatisfied with the product or apathetic about its future that they've just given it away. Google any combination of the words *the church in decline*, and you'll find alarming statistics. The COVID-19 pandemic had an effect, but the decline had been going on for years before that event.

A Gallup poll taken recently found that for the first time in eight decades Americans' membership in houses of worship dropped below 50 percent. Only 47 percent of adults in the United States claim to be a member of a church, mosque, or synagogue, a 23-point decline since 2000.

According to that study, about one-in-three (34 percent) of Americans in 2019 attended worship one-to-two times per month. Today, that figure is creeping closer to one-in-four (28 percent)—a decline of six percent.[2]

Put simply, if you have stock in the church, your broker might be telling you to sell it, not buy more.

Before we throw in the towel or wave the white flag of surrender, however, let's read how Paul concludes his first prison prayer: "God placed all things under [Christ's] feet and appointed him to be head over everything for the church, which is his body, the fullness of him who fills everything in every way" (Ephesians 1:22-23).

Jesus had no sooner taken his seat at the right hand of the Father than God immediately placed everything under his feet and made him the head over everything for the church. And I emphasize those last three words—*for the church*.

Writing about Ephesians 1:20-23, Tim Keller wrote,

> Notice that little word *for*. Ephesians 1 is saying that the man who died for you is now not only at the right hand of the divine throne but he's there as the executive director of history, directing everything for the benefit of the church. If you belong to him, then everything that happens, ultimately happens for you.[3]

The church is not a building; it's Christ's body, and he and he alone is the head of that body. So remember this: *It's not our church; it's his church.* And he's in charge of *his* church. He's also ultimately responsible for the future of *his* church. He's the one who said, "The gates of Hades will not overcome it" (Matthew 16:18).

Now, consider how Paul said the church enjoys "the fullness of him who fills everything in every way" (Ephesians 1:23). This is a challenging verse to translate from the Greek, and Bible scholars vary on its exact meaning, but it states both that Jesus Christ is the head of the church and that he fills the church. He fills it with his fullness with everything the church needs in every way. Jesus takes care of his body!

Ultimately, and even eternally, the church is not only in the heart of Jesus but in the hands of Jesus. He holds the supreme position of the church, and he is the supernatural power in the church. He's not only over us, his church, but in us. He's not only the leader of the church, his church, but the Lord over us.

This is why we need to recapture and remember this thought, really letting it sink in: *It's not our church, it's his church.* The reason you should be committed to a local church is that you're coming to Christ's body, not to just a building. And you're a part of that body. Furthermore, although our physical bodies are vulnerable to disease and death—or at least stock challenges—Christ's body is not. The church is the only entity in the entire world that will last forever. It's the only entity that will be in heaven.

This is why we should pray for the church—for my church and for your church. We should go to the God who hears, asking that every church be filled with the fullness of Jesus. At the end of the day, what should bring people to church and ultimately keep them there is not plans and programs but the person and the power of Jesus.

The late celebrity chef Anthony Bourdain once said, "[It's a place] where everybody, regardless of race, creed, color or degree of inebriation, is welcomed.

Its warm, yellow glow, a beacon of hope and salvation, inviting the hungry, the lost, the seriously hammered all across the South to come inside. A place of safety and nourishment. It never closes. It is always faithful, always there for you."[4] Too bad he was writing about Waffle House rather than the church, but perhaps his mention of inebriation should have been a clue!

I honestly believe that description is the call of every church, made possible when it is truly filled with the fullness of Jesus. Romans 15:7 says to accept one another "just as Christ accepted you, in order to bring praise to God."

Father, thank you for the church, whose future is eternally bright because the head of the church is the Lord Jesus Christ. Thank you that I'm a part of his church, his body, and I pray that both my church and I will be filled with his fullness, bringing praise to you. Amen.

EPHESIANS 3:14-21

I kneel before the Father, from whom every family in heaven and on earth derives its name. I pray that out of his glorious riches he may strengthen you with power through his Spirit in your inner being, so that Christ may dwell in your hearts through faith. And I pray that you, being rooted and established in love, may have power, together with all the Lord's holy people, to grasp how wide and long and high and deep is the love of Christ, and to know this love that surpasses knowledge—that you may be filled to the measure of all the fullness of God.

Now to him who is able to do immeasurably more than all we ask or imagine, according to his power that is at work within us, to him be glory in the church and in Christ Jesus throughout all generations, for ever and ever! Amen.

11

BEFORE YOU PRAY

*The only time my prayers are never
answered is on the golf course.*[1]

BILLY GRAHAM

Now we come to Paul's next prison prayer, moving from Ephesians 1
to Ephesians 3.

You might be baffled by the quote above from Billy Graham,
thinking, *What in the world does golf have to do with prayer?* But for me, golf
has a great deal to do with prayer.

Let me explain. After years of resisting entreaties from friends and church
members, I finally gave in to trying golf. And once I did, I caught what's called
"the golf bug." That bug didn't just bite me, though, causing my affliction. It
devoured me!

Now, if you're a golfer, you'll appreciate this, and if you're not, beware
before you take up the game. Golf is the most exhilarating and yet frustrat-
ing game I've ever played in my life. When you make a great shot, you want
to praise God. But when you make a bad one, you want to curse the devil.
And unless you're a pro, your bad shots will probably outnumber your good

ones—and they can be *bad*. Trust me, the heavens really can seem to turn to brass on the golf course (Deuteronomy 28:23).

A number of years ago I was blessed to connect with a teaching pro who is one of the best in the business. He has worked with a former British Open champion, which tells you something about his expertise, and I affectionately and teasingly call him Lipper. (His real last name is Lipnick. When you've "lipped out," your golf ball hits the lip of the cup but doesn't drop into the hole. That has nothing to do with his nickname, but it is appropriate for many of my putts!)

After he watched my swing for a while, I asked him to go ahead and tell me what I was doing wrong. With a grin, he said, "Oh, I never teach that way. I always start with the positives, so let's talk about what you're doing right."

Encouraged and after a sigh of relief, I said, "Great. Tell me what I'm doing right, then."

Then, with his grin turned devilish, he let me have it. "Nothing!"

He wasn't kidding.

For my first lesson, Lipper taught me three letters—GPA, which stand for *grip*, *posture*, and *alignment*—and I'll never forget what he said next, because it's proven to be true for me: "Almost every problem in golf relates to one of those three things. Either your grip is wrong, your posture is wrong, or your alignment is wrong." Over the years, I've returned to Lipper many times for what golfers call "tune-ups," especially when my game really gets out of whack. And guess what? My problem almost always was traced to one of those three issues.

So I've learned that what you do before you swing is as important, if not more important, as your actual swing. No matter how good your swing is, if your grip is off, or your posture is off, or your alignment is off, your golf game will be off.

The same is true in prayer. Before you can pray effectively, you need to make sure of three things:

1. That you have a *good grip* on your personal relationship with God through your daily walk with Jesus.

2. That you go to God with a *posture of submission* to his authority over your life.

3. That you're *aligned* in the direction he wants your life to go, according to the truths found in his Word.

Studying this prison prayer of Paul's will teach you how to make sure those fundamentals are in place and help enforce them through prayer because that is what this prayer is all about. In fact, the more you study this prayer and pray as Paul prayed, the more you'll realize the apostle's grip, posture, and alignment could not have been better.

Again, he wrote this letter to the Ephesians while imprisoned, but unlike those of us who tend to pray most for what we want and what we need, he wasn't praying for himself. In fact, his prayer had nothing to do with what he wanted God to do for him. It had to do with what he wanted God to do in him and in the church at Ephesus.

Just the way Paul begins this part of his letter should get our attention: "I kneel before the Father" (Ephesians 3:14). We'll get into the several postures of prayer in the next devotion, but whenever someone is driven to their knees in prayer, they are not praying a *Now I lay me down to sleep* or *Thank you for this food* or *Bless me today* prayer, as genuine as they are. They are entering a time of prayer with a real grip on God. They are communicating that they are in a posture of complete submission to whatever he wants even before they pray. And they are making it clear to him that they want to be aligned with his direction in their life's journey.

Ephesians 3:14-21 has impacted my life more than I can say. I've memorized these verses—the only ones other than the Lord's Prayer—personalizing them and making them my first prayer before I begin each day. This strengthens my grip on God like nothing else, puts me in the right posture from the start, and helps me submit to whatever God wants me to do and wherever he wants me to go. And by also desiring that my will be in perfect alignment with God's, he gives me a peace and joy I can't explain.

So before you pray, remember GPA. Be sure of your grip, posture, and alignment before you approach the God who hears, and then you'll be ready.

Lord, before I pray, I want my grip on you to be strong. I want my heart in a posture of total submission to whatever you desire to do in me and with me. And may everyone who follows behind me today see that my life is in alignment with your will and your Word. Bless me now as I begin to pray in your name, amen.

POSTURE MATTERS

*There are moments, when, whatever the posture
of the body, the soul is on its knees.*[1]

VICTOR HUGO

Perhaps you've heard this story, though a few details might be different. Three seminary professors were standing in a hallway discussing the best posture for prayer while a man repairing an electrical problem worked on his task nearby.

One of the theologians said, "I believe the best posture for prayer is kneeling. It shows humility."

Another one said, "I believe the best position is lying prostrate face down on the floor. That shows complete submission."

And then the last theologian said, "Well, I believe the best posture is standing with your hands outstretched toward heaven. That shows willingness to receive whatever God wants to give you."

Suddenly, the man making the repair jumped into the conversation. "The best praying I ever did was when I was hanging upside down from a utility pole!"

This joke is funny, but it also raises a good question. How important is posture in prayer? We hear a lot about what to pray for, but we don't hear too much about what posture or position we should take when we pray. Yet Paul seemed to want the Ephesians to specifically know that as he was praying this prayer on their behalf, he was doing it in a particular posture of prayer—on bended knees. "I kneel before the Father," he told them.

Have you ever wondered why Paul shared what posture he took as he prayed for them? I have. Paul was a Jew, and even today, if you have the opportunity to visit the Wailing Wall in Jerusalem, you'll see devout Orthodox Jews standing and rocking back and forth as they pray, just as in my earlier story about the old man praying there. The Jewish people rarely kneel when they pray, nor did they in Paul's time.

The Ephesians were Gentile by birth (Ephesians 2:11), but they knew Paul was Jewish. So here's why I think he told them he kneeled when he prayed for them: He wanted them to know this prayer he strongly felt led to pray on their behalf was so earthshaking, revolutionary, and life changing that it drove him, a Jew, to his knees. Up in verses 2 and 3 of this chapter, he even told the Ephesians, "Surely you have heard about the administration of God's grace *that was given to me for you*, that is, the mystery made known to me by revelation."

God is more concerned with the petition of our prayers than the posture we take when we pray. What we say with our lips is important to him, of course, but our body language counts too. Our bodies can express on the outside what our hearts are experiencing on the inside. (A good example is how my whole body shakes whenever the University of Georgia football team is about to win—and then does!)

Still, the Bible repeatedly mentions postures taken in prayer, indicating several we can take as well. John MacArthur notes a number of them:

- Standing (Genesis 24:12-14)
- Lifting the hands (1 Timothy 2:8)

- Sitting (Judges 20:26)

- Kneeling (Mark 1:40)

- Looking upward (John 17:1)

- Bowing down (Exodus 34:8)

- Placing the head between the knees (1 Kings 18:42)

- Pounding on the breast (Luke 18:13)

- Facing the temple (Daniel 6:10)[2]

The point of posture is simply that when we pray, we should throw our whole selves into it. We should be totally involved—body, soul, mind, and spirit. It really is important to the God who hears that we express our love, devotion, reverence, desire, awe, and need of him by not only what we say but by how we say it.

The only other prayer I have totally memorized besides the Lord's Prayer is this one. The more I studied it, meditated on it, and repeated it, the more deeply it impacted my heart.

At times I am sure you are like me when you feel that your prayers are like throwing stuff against the wall and hoping it sticks. I can assure you that you will know from the get-go this one always sticks! Let me encourage you not to just study this prayer in the following chapters but to memorize it and begin to pray it every day. I can honestly say that if you pray it daily, believe it totally, and live it consistently, you cannot help but see a difference in your prayer life. As you do keep this in mind: *We don't always get what we pray for, but we always get what God wants us to pray for.* This is a one-size-fits-all prayer you can pray for anybody, anywhere, anytime, under any circumstances, knowing you will never pray a better prayer than this one for you and for them. So why not start today in a posture of submission and expectation, knowing God will certainly answer this prayer!

Heavenly Father, as I pray, in my heart I'm in a posture of praise before you, and as I think of all you've done for me, all you mean to me, and all you are to me, I'm driven to gratitude and love. I may not always get what I pray for, but I rest in the assurance I'll always get what you want me to pray for and use this prayer to teach me that always. Thank you. Amen.

13

IN THE FAMILY

As a child of God…you have the collective strength and excellence
of your spiritual family—your true family of origin.[1]

MARK BATTERSON

When my three sons were small, either Teresa or I would drive them to school. I miss those days. They were some of the sweetest times of fun, laughter, and fellowship my kids and I had together, although at the same time I had to encourage them to want to go to school because none of them did!

Before they left the car, we'd pray together, and then I'd say, "Remember who you are and who you belong to." And they would say, "I'm a Merritt, and I belong to God." Whenever I take my grandchildren to school, I say exactly the same thing to them.

Knowing who you are and who you belong to is vitally important to your prayer life. When Paul writes, "I kneel before the Father, from whom every family in heaven and on earth derives its name" (Ephesians 3:14-15), he reminds the Ephesians and us of two things we need to remember as we pray—the *fatherhood* of God and the *family* of God.

Prayer is a family affair. When we pray, we're not at an appointment with a business, negotiating a contract, or completing an application for some kind of assistance. We're coming as a family member into the presence of the Holy God who created this world, and even more into the presence of the Father who has adopted us into his family.

It's interesting that God is referred to as Father in the Old Testament only 14 times.[2] But even a cursory reading through the Gospels shows us that "Father" is the term Jesus favored when addressing God. In the Synoptic Gospels alone (the books of Matthew, Mark, and Luke), Jesus uses "Father" when referring to God 65 times, and in the Gospel of John he uses it more than a hundred times.

Now, the word "Father" sounds rather formal, but keep in mind that the Gospels in Greek translate nearly all of Jesus' use of the word "Father" into *Pater*, which means father. But Jesus spoke Aramaic, and in Mark 14:36 he used the word *Abba*, which is more akin to our English word "Daddy." It's a word little children would have used to refer to their earthly father, just as they do today.[3] If we picture prayer as talking to God as a child would talk to their dad, it might not only motivate us to pray more but to pray longer.

I'm reminded of the story about a pastor who called the children of his church up front on Sunday mornings to give them an illustration. For one service he brought up a cell phone to help explain prayer.

He began, "We all know that when you talk to someone on a cell phone, you can't see them while you're talking. Right?"

The children all nodded.

"Well," the pastor continued, "talking to God is like talking on a cell phone. He's on the other end of the connection, and you can't see him, but he's listening to every word."

One boy piped up and said, "What's his number?"

But we don't need a number. When anyone who by faith in the Son of the Father becomes a part of the Father's family, God is with us. Just as we should talk to him as we would talk to a dad, he listens to us just like a dad should listen to his children. This is what Paul meant when he wrote, "From whom every family in heaven and on earth derives its name." He was referring to God's children of every age, whether Old Testament saints or New Testament saints, whether Jews or Gentiles, whether alive on this earth or in heaven. We are always in the family, never apart from the family, and we are to pray to the Father and for one another as members of the family.

So be encouraged! You may not be known by the world. You may feel insignificant. You may feel as if you're totally forgotten. But if you're a Christian, God is your Father, and you're in his family. You always have complete, total, unfiltered access to the Father who knows your every need and loves you like no earthly parent ever could.

It's common for people to bet on a horse based on its bloodline, and here's how these bloodlines came about in racing:

> Thoroughbred horses are a breed of horse that trace their origins back
> to three key sires, or "father" horses: Darley Arabian, Godolphin
> Arabian, and Byerly Turk. The owners, for whom the horses are
> named, transported the horses to England from the Middle East
> in the late 17th and early 18th century…Bulle Rock, son of Darley
> Arabian, was the first thoroughbred in America. Brought to Virginia
> in 1730, he had already been a successful racehorse for many years
> in Britain. By the year 1800, more than 300 thoroughbreds had
> followed him to America.[4]

That's interesting, but I have news for you that's more than good. You are a divine thoroughbred. You are a royal blueblood. As God's children, we trace our spiritual bloodline to the one and only King of kings and Lord of lords! And so we should all be moved to prayer and to stay in prayer knowing that we're talking to the Father who not only hears but has adopted us into his family forever.

Father, may I never get over the fact that you are my Father and that's what you want me to call you. Thank you for making me your child. Wherever I go today, may I remember who I am and to whom I belong. In the name of your Son, amen.

POWER SURGE

With the power of God within us,
we need never fear the powers around us.[1]
WOODROW KROLL

A question came to me via email from a man in our church: *Why do we not see a showcase of the power of God transforming people's lives more than we do?*

Talk about a tough question! But after some serious thinking, this is what I concluded: The power of God is too often missing from the lives of Christians because they don't believe God the way he deserves to be believed, obey God the way he demands to be obeyed, and love God the way he desires to be loved. It's beyond dispute that if they did—if we all did—the body of Christ would look radically different.

The apostle Peter wrote, "His divine power has given us everything we need for a godly life through our knowledge of him who called us by his own glory and goodness" (2 Peter 1:3), but we have to believe, obey, and love God as he would have us believe, obey, and love him. In his first letter to the Corinthians, Paul implored them to "live in a right way in undivided devotion to the Lord" (1 Corinthians 7:35).

I honestly believe that if we asked God for what Paul asked on behalf of the church in Ephesus and then lived believing God granted what we asked, we would see his transforming power unleashed both in our lives personally and in our churches corporately as never before.

We know Paul was incredibly moved by the power of this prayer…because it drove him to his knees. And we know he prayed in a way most of us rarely begin our prayers…for someone else. But the apostle also begins not by asking God to do something *for* the Christians in Ephesus but by asking him to do something *in* them: "I pray that out of his glorious riches he may strengthen you with power through his Spirit in your inner being" (Ephesians 3:16).

Paul prayed for what I call God's power surge in their lives, and I believe I know why. He knew that unless they were daily and continuously strengthened in God's power by his Holy Spirit, they could never really walk with, work for, witness for, or even worship God the way they should. This is true for all of us. Only the power of God enables us to live for the God of all power.

In John Stott's book *Basic Christianity*, he gives a great illustration for this principle, which I've briefly adapted here. If someone asked you to write a play like Shakespeare's *Romeo and Juliet*, you couldn't. Likewise, if someone asked you to live a life like Jesus did, you couldn't. But if you somehow absorbed the genius of Shakespeare inside of you, you could write a play like he did. Likewise, when the Spirit of God lives in you, you have the power to live a life like Jesus did.[2]

One of the excuses I hear from people who refuse to follow Jesus goes something like this: "I could never live up to the Christian life." Well, they're right. No one can live up to the Christian life on their own, and God has never asked anyone to even try it. In his book *The Indwelling Life of Christ*, Major Ian Thomas wrote, "I cannot—God never said I could." And then he added, "But God can, and always said He would!"[3]

Paul's first prayer was not for health or wealth. It wasn't to find a "get out of jail free" card or have favor with a judge or a jury, and it had nothing to do with what God could do for him, but rather what God could do in him. He prayed for God's power surge in his life. Paul was not praying for what was happening on the outside of that prison, but what was happening on the inside of him. I do not believe it was at all coincidental that this was the first thing he prayed for.

This is why I think asking for God's power goes to the top of Paul's list in this prayer. The only way anyone can do the will of God is through the power received from the Holy Spirit working in them. Life is a battle and full of burdens, but we're not in it alone.

I love this story about a man who ran off a country road, his car careening into a ditch. Not only had his cell phone died, but he hardly knew where he was. A farmer came by in a horse-drawn wagon, but he didn't have a cell phone with him, and the nearest towing service was about 50 miles away.

"Honestly," the farmer said, "we need a team of horses to pull out your car. But let's see what Dusty here can do even though he's old and blind and believe God for the best."

The farmer hitched Dusty to the car, then cracked a whip in the air and shouted, "Pull, Jimmy, pull!" Jimmy? The horse didn't move. The farmer snapped the whip two more times, each time calling Dusty by yet another name—Sam and then Charlie. The horse remained totally still both times. Then the farmer snapped the whip a fourth time and shouted, "Pull, Dusty, pull!" With one mighty tug from Dusty, that car was out of the ditch.

The driver was grateful, but he had a question. "Why didn't you just call him Dusty from the start? That *is* his name, right?"

"Yes. But remember that Dusty is blind, which means he can't be positive whether he's the only horse here or has company. But if he'd thought he had to pull your car out by himself, he wouldn't have even attempted the task."

We don't face the barriers of life, carry the burdens of life, or fight the battles of life on our own. We have at our disposal the power of God through the Holy Spirit in our inner being. It's ours for the asking and taking.

Heavenly Father, I pray that in my inner being you will strengthen me with your power through your Holy Spirit. I know that with that power, no barrier can stop me, no battle will defeat me, and no burden will break me. In the name of the One who hears my prayer, amen.

RIGHT AT HOME

Home is where the heart is.

PROVERB

once received a precious letter from a woman whose son-in-law was a surgeon. At the time, his two children—his son, Zac, and his daughter, Madison—were quite young.

One day he returned home from an emergency surgery, and Zac wanted to know all about it. "Dad, did you have to cut the man open to see what was inside of him?"

"Yes, son."

Zac's eyes widened. "Could you see things like his lungs and his stomach?"

"Yes, I could."

"And could you see his heart?"

That's when Madison jumped in. "Did you see Jesus in his heart, Dad?"

From a child comes a really good question!

Christians often refer to salvation as the moment a person asks Jesus "to come into their heart." That's exactly what I did as a nine-year-old boy sitting in a movie theater in Gainesville, Georgia, watching the film *King of Kings* with my mother and older brother. I asked Jesus to come into my heart and be my Lord and Savior.

At the moment of salvation, every believer experiences Christ coming to live inside them in the person of the Holy Spirit (2 Corinthians 13:5; Colossians 1:27; Romans 8:9-10). Someone even pithily described Christianity as *Christ-in-you-ity*. I think this is why in the next part of Paul's prayer, he says something that might have seemed strange to the Christians in Ephesus.

He's just said he prays that they will be strengthened with power by God's Spirit in their inner being, and then he tells them the reason he does—"so that Christ may dwell in your hearts through faith" (Ephesians 3:17). This is the only place in the Bible that speaks of Jesus dwelling—or living—in our hearts, so it's interesting that this description of salvation is so common among Christians today.

Now, at first it seems as though Paul has put the cart before the horse because no one can receive the Holy Spirit apart from first receiving Christ. The Holy Spirit brings us to Jesus, and then Jesus gives us the Holy Spirit. But upon further examination, we can see why this part of Paul's prayer is so vital to the Christian life.

The word Paul uses here for "dwell" is one of two similar Greek words used for "dwelling." One word is *paroikeo*, which simply means "to inhabit a place as a stranger." It would be more like a bed-and-breakfast or an Airbnb, where you might stay for a night or two but never settle down.[1] The other word Paul uses—*katoikeo*—is much more powerful. It combines the words for "down" and "house" and refers to a place where you want to settle down and never leave—a place where you feel "right at home."[2]

Ask yourself this question: *Does Jesus feel right at home in my heart?* This is far different from asking if Jesus is in your heart. There's a difference between his being in the house of your heart, which happens upon conversion, and his feeling at home in your heart, an ongoing process. Steven J. Cole writes about "Christ's taking up residence in us in a deeper, more conscious way than we experience at conversion."[3]

When I have guests in my home, as soon as they walk in the door I tell them, "I want you to feel right at home because our home is now yours. We don't have guests or friends; we have family members." Hopefully, your desire is to ensure your heart is a place where Jesus feels right at home. But what does that really mean? Answer these questions honestly:

- Does Jesus have access to every room in your heart? Or are any off-limits because you don't want him to see what's there or what you do there?

- Does Jesus have the head seat at the table in your heart? Or is he asked to sit in a corner with his chair facing a wall? Are you in control of the agenda and the menu, not he?

The only home Jesus feels at home in is the one where he has complete control.

Evangelist Francis Dixon wrote, "This is…what we must do with the Lord who has come to live in our hearts. He must have the freedom to go through the hall, into the dining-room, the lounge, the bedrooms, or out into the garden."[4]

Here's one more question: Is Jesus allowed to sleep in the master bedroom of your heart (pun intended)? Because in reality, when he comes to live inside us, Jesus is not a guest. He's our owner. And who should feel more at home in a house than its owner?

If you asked Jesus if he feels right at home in your heart, how do you think he would answer? And if he said no, what steps would you take to make him feel at home? I believe Stephen Cole was right when he said, "To make Christ at home in your heart, you need prayer, power through God's Spirit, and faith."[5] Start there. And remember, when you pray and believe God hears, he does.

Lord Jesus, through prayer, power through God's Spirit, and faith, I give you access to every room in the house of my heart. You have the head seat at the table, and you will sleep in the master bedroom. For home is where the heart is when the heart is truly your home. In your name I pray, amen.

FIRM AND DEEP

I have given God countless reasons not to love me.
None of them has been strong enough to change Him.[1]

PAUL WASHER

D o you know what a building and a tree have in common—especially tall ones? You can't see it, at least not without extra effort, but it's certainly important to their survival.

You see, if we want to build a tall building that will last, we have to start with a deep foundation. And for a tree to grow tall and survive, it must have a strong, deep root system. Yet most of us never visit the 104-story One World Trade Center in New York City to view its foundation or go to Yosemite National Park to examine the roots of the Sequoias. We tend to look at the trunks of trees and not their roots and admire the majesty of buildings reaching toward the sky and ignore their bases. We're impressed by super-tall skyscrapers and super-tall trees because of their height, but what really ought to impress us is their depth.

The same thing is true when we look at people. We forget that the strength of a person and their true character are revealed not by what we see above ground but what's below ground (or what's on the inside, not the outside). And what makes the difference is love—God's love.

I believe the next part of Paul's prayer is the master key to living the Christian life: "I pray that you, being rooted and established in love…" (Ephesians 3:17). And I don't think it's coincidental that he uses both an agricultural term—*rooted*—and an architectural term—*established*—to illustrate just how vital this love is.

Our lives are to be rooted deep in the soil of God's love, and they're to be built on the firm foundation of his love. The love from above gives us the strength to deal with difficult people, and the love from above gives us the stability to weather challenges. And the deeper we go in our love for God, the higher we go for the glory of God.

To be rooted in love is even more important than what we say we believe, because whatever captures our heart will control our feelings and behavior. As Tim Keller noted in one of his books, people "change not merely by changing their thinking but by changing what they love most."[2] What your heart loves the most, your mind will reason out, your emotions will feel out, and your will shall act out.

There simply is no power that can strengthen us like the power of God's love. The ultimate display of this power was, of course, at the cross. Romans 5:8 reminds us, "God demonstrates his own love for us in this: While we were still sinners, Christ died for us." I read this somewhere, and it stuck with me: Roman soldiers put Jesus on the cross, but love kept him there.

One of the reasons the church has so many problems today (and that people have so many problems with the church) is that our roots have shrunk and our foundations have cracked. It's little wonder that the people of the world don't love one another the way they should when even fellow believers so often don't love one another the way we should.

We need to ask God to make us individually rooted and grounded in his love, and then ask that all Christians in Christ's church will be corporately rooted and grounded in God's love as well. Only God's love truly binds churches, families, and friends together. The apostle Peter said it best: "Above all, love each other deeply, because love covers over a multitude of sins" (1 Peter 4:8).

When lives are truly rooted and grounded in God's love, families will never fracture, friendships will never fail, churches will never divide, and even enemies will be turned into friends.

I want to share this thought-provoking observation Episcopalian priest Wes Seeliger made in his book *One Church from the Fence*:

> I have spent long hours in the intensive care waiting room…watching with anguished people…listening to urgent questions: Will my husband make it? Will my child walk again? How do you live without your companion of thirty years? The intensive care waiting room is different from any other place in the world. And the people who wait are different. They can't do enough for each other. No one is rude. The distinctions of race and class melt away. A person is a father first, a black man second. The garbage man loves his wife as much as the university professor loves his, and everyone understands this. Each person pulls for everyone else.
>
> In the intensive care waiting room, the world changes. Vanity and pretense vanish. The universe is focused on the doctor's next report. If only it will show improvement. Everyone knows that loving someone else is what life is all about.[3]

If we realized that every day is a day in the waiting room, could we learn to love like that? This world desperately needs to see Christians truly following Jesus with lives that are rooted and grounded in his love. So as you examine your own life, ask yourself these two simple questions: *How firm is my foundation?* and *How deep are my roots?*

God of love, may my life be rooted and grounded in the love that only you can give. May I always remember that the deeper I go in loving you, the higher I will go in glorifying you. And may people see in me, hear from me, and experience with me your love. In Jesus' name I pray, amen.

UNLIMITED AND UNSURPASSED

God's love is like an ocean.
You can see its beginning, but not its end.[1]

RICK WARREN

'll never forget the elation I felt the day my first child was born, holding my own flesh and blood, knowing that God had brought him into this world through the love my beautiful wife, Teresa, and I shared. Rarely have I felt such an indescribable and overwhelming emotion. I had experienced the love a child has for a parent, but when I held this son for the first time, I experienced the love of a parent for a child.

Decades later, I had the experience of watching that son hold his first child, a son of his own. With my arms around his shoulders, I told him, "Now you know how much your mom and I love you."

It's a wonderful thing to experience real love, to feel what love from another human being is like. But there's a love so great, so powerful, so unique, and so different that it requires the power of the One who gives us that love to even try to grasp it. The love of God is different from the love of humanity in that it truly is unlimited, unsurpassed, and unending.

Perhaps the most popular Christian children's song ever written is the one that simply says "Jesus loves me! This I know." Here's a staggering truth: We know Jesus loves us, but we have no real idea how great that love is.

The next thing Paul writes in Ephesians 3 is both inspiring and challenging. He says he prays that the Christians in Ephesus will "have power together with all the Lord's holy people, to grasp how wide and long and high and deep is the love of Christ" (Ephesians 3:18). This part of the prayer actually goes hand in hand with the previous part, "I pray that you, being rooted and established in love…" (verse 17). Paul prayed for them to be rooted and grounded in love, to live lives built on a foundation of love for God and from God. We too, then, should continuously ask God to help us truly know and be confident in his unparalleled love for us.

Oswald Chambers said, "The love of God is not created—it is His nature."[2] And C.S. Lewis wrote, "God loves us not because we're lovable, because He is love. Not because He needs to receive, because He delights to give."[3] Here, Paul speaks of God's love in four dimensions, which may be making an even greater statement than we realize.

We're three-dimensional beings who live in a three-dimensional world. Time is made up of past, present, and future. Space is made up of height, length, and width. Matter is made up of solid, liquid, and gas. But God's love surpasses all earthly dimensions. It's a four-dimensional love. This means no one loves you or can love you the way God does. No one.

- God's love is so *wide* that he can love everyone in the entire world. His love plays no favorites. He loves everyone equally and unconditionally.

- God's love is so *long* that it lasts forever. He will never stop loving anyone. Someone once said a sinner may go to hell unsaved, but he will not go to hell unloved. God's love is an eternal love.

- God's love is so *high* that it can enable every human to climb the mountain toward heaven and take them to its very peak.

- God's love is so *deep* that it can reach down into the heart of the most wicked person the human mind can imagine and change that heart forever.

You don't have to ask God to love you. After all, God *is* love. But on a daily basis he wants us, along with all of his people, to pray for the power to even begin to grasp just how great his love for us is.

Do you know when you most need to remember God's great love? When you go through those dark times of the soul, when a debilitating disease or a devastating death or a disappointing defeat tempts you to doubt his love. When that happens, ask him to give you the power to wrap your loving arms around him, believing that he always has his loving arms wrapped around you. He will hold on to you even when you're tempted to let go of him.

We're told that Frederick M. Lehman, born in Germany in 1868, did that very thing during a difficult time in his life. After losing his business, he became so destitute that he ended up packing oranges and lemons on a farm. He was beginning to wonder if God cared about him at all. Then he attended a church service and heard a sermon on the love of God. He made up his mind that God did indeed love him, and the next morning on a piece of scrap paper, he began writing his hymn "The Love of God."

Here are the lyrics from the third stanza, which he wrote after remembering a poem found written on a prison wall. I've included the hymn's refrain as well.

Could we with ink the ocean fill,
and were the skies of parchment made;
were ev'ry stalk on earth a quill,
and ev'ryone a scribe by trade;
to write the love of God above
would drain the ocean dry;
nor could the scroll contain the whole,
though stretched from sky to sky

Refrain:
O love of God, how rich and pure!
How measureless and strong!
It shall forevermore endure—
the saints' and angels' song.[4]

This is the love God has for you—unlimited, unsurpassed, and unending.

God, I really have no earthly idea how much you love me, but I ask that you give me the divine power to know that your love from above is greater than any love that can ever come from here below. Amen.

IT'S BEYOND ME

Knowing what you don't know is more useful than being brilliant.[1]
CHARLIE MUNGER

We live in strange times, don't we? On the one hand, because of computerization, globalization, and innovation, not since the world began has its people had access to so much knowledge about so many things. A 2021 article quoted, "Not only is human knowledge, on average, doubling every 13 months, [but] we are quickly on our way, with the help of the Internet, to the doubling of knowledge every 12 hours. To put it into context, in 1900 human knowledge doubled approximately every 100 years. By the end of 1945, the rate was every 25 years."[2]

Now, when you think about it, what this really means is not that we're learning how much we know; we're learning how much we don't know. This quote is attributed to several humorists, including Mark Twain, but whoever said it was right: "It ain't what you don't know that gets you into trouble. It's what you know for sure that just ain't so."[3] As our knowledge increases, we're beginning to realize that what we thought were facts are no longer facts. This can be unsettling and cause mistakes, but here's why it's true. Attributed to economist Fritz Machlup, the term *half-life of knowledge* is the time that passes before half the knowledge or facts in a particular area are made obsolete or are superseded by new knowledge or facts. As our knowledge explodes, facts change. And that's why we now know the earth isn't flat, smoking is bad for you, and Pluto isn't a planet. Did you know a swallowed piece of gum doesn't really take seven years to digest?[4]

But we can absolutely be sure of one thing about God, and as strange as this sounds, it's also one thing we can never know about him. It's expressed in what Bible scholars rightly call an oxymoron and found in Paul's words in Ephesians 3:19. He says he prays that God will give the church at Ephesus the power to "know this love [of Christ] that surpasses knowledge."

We can know that Jesus loves us, although in our last devotion we talked about how we can't really grasp just how great that love is. But how are we supposed to know anything about his love if it's beyond our human knowledge? Furthermore, how are we supposed to know how *much* he loves us?

I know beyond a shadow of a doubt that Jesus loves me, but I also know beyond a shadow of a doubt that I don't know how much he loves me. It's beyond me because of who he is and how he loves. And it's so unlike any other love we will ever experience. For example, I love my wife, but I'm not love, and I'm certainly not always as loving toward her or loveable as I should be. But Jesus *is* love, and he's always loving and loveable.

And so we should pray that we will experience the great love of Jesus even when we can't fully comprehend it nor how much he loves us with our minds, no matter how fast earthly knowledge increases. Neither on this side of heaven nor when we're there will we be able to truly understand God's love for us nor how much he loves us, so never think you do or will. It's forever beyond us.

That's true even though the New Living Translation of the Bible uses these words for 1 John 4:9: "God showed *how much he loved us* by sending his one and only Son into the world so that we might have eternal life through him." For Christians, recognizing and accepting the miraculous gift of salvation is only the beginning of knowing how much God loves us.

Another great hymn, "My Savior's Love," has a refrain with these words:

> How marvelous! How wonderful!
> And my song shall ever be;
> How marvelous! How wonderful!
> Is my Savior's love for me![5]

I know I don't love God anywhere near as much as he loves me, and in this case, ignorance is bliss. What a wonderful thought that the great love Jesus has for us is so wide and long and deep and high that we will never be able to fully comprehend it!

I'm inspired by these words from Corrie ten Boom:

> When we are on the beach we see only a small part of the ocean.
> However, we know that there is much more beyond the horizon.
> We only see a small part of God's love, a few jewels of his great
> riches, but we know that there is much more beyond the horizon.
> The best is yet to come, when we see Jesus face-to-face.[6]

"Jesus loves me, this I know, for the Bible tells me so,"[7] but not even the Bible fully expresses in words just how much he loves us. God's love is still beyond human description and comprehension, and that fact alone should make us fall more in love with him every day.

Sometimes you may doubt the wisdom of God, the works of God, and the ways of God, but never doubt the love of the God who hears. He loves you more than you will ever know!

Lord Jesus, thank you for loving me with a love I will never fully comprehend, because although your love may surpass my mind, I know it will never bypass my heart. Amen.

COMPLETELY FULL

God can't fill you when you are full of yourself.
AUTHOR UNKNOWN

Before you even board a plane, more often than not you'll hear five words that sound like courtesy information: "This flight is completely full." But beware. In my opinion, those words communicate a dire warning.

If you're a seasoned traveler, you're automatically alerted to two somber facts. First, there's no chance you'll have an empty seat next to you, so you'll be fighting for elbow room the entire flight, especially if you're assigned a middle seat. Second, if you have a piece of carry-on luggage, you better get on the plane as fast as you can or the bins will run out of room and you'll have to check it, which is a hassle. Plus, you always risk your checked baggage somehow disappearing. But what to me is a dire warning is to the airline a happy fact. No seat was ever installed in a plane to stay empty.

To God, you're like a commercial airline. He wants you to be completely full—but full of *him*. He wants to fill every nook and cranny of you and your life with his power and his presence. So when you truly come to know the love of God that surpasses all human knowledge and experience the incomparable love God has for you, you should want nothing more than to be completely filled with the fullness of God himself.

This is why the next part of Paul's prayer for the Ephesian church is not just theologically magnificent but logically expected. What Christian wouldn't want to be "filled to the measure of all the fullness of God" (Ephesians 3:19)?

Back as far as 1600, someone coined the phrase *full of oneself*.[1] It's still used today to describe people who are so conceited, egotistical, and self-centered that they have "an exaggerated sense of self-importance."[2]

I know people like that. Don't you? And I confess that sometimes I'm guilty of not seeing anyone but me, not caring about anyone but me, and not loving anyone more than I love me. When that happens, what's most important to me is...well, me. And generally speaking, at any given moment we're either full of God or full of ourselves because we can't be half full of God and half full of self. God doesn't share spiritual space with anyone.

Frankly, the theologians I read admit that they, like me, aren't quite sure what Ephesians 3:19 means. One commentary, however, says, "The fullness of God is the totality of everything God is—His attributes, His character, His perfection, His holiness, His power, His love, et cetera. The fullness of God is His complete nature; it is who He is."[3]

How do we fathom being filled with all the fullness of God when even the universe can't contain him (1 Kings 8:27)? Yet we should daily ask God to receive his fullness from top to bottom, from north to south, and from east to west, asking for his help to live in such a way that his fullness overflows into the lives of others.

When you're full of something, it dominates you, and we should pray to be so full of God that people see in us his love, hear from us his voice, and experience through us His presence.

Do you know what free diving is? It's swimming "beneath the surface of the water especially at considerable depth without a portable breathing device."[4] An article I found gives this interesting fact about free diving as well as a piece of advice:

> On 27 March 2021...Budimir Šobat from Croatia at the age of 56 years old broke the record of the longest dive in one breath at 24 minutes, 37.36 seconds.

Wow. Then it says,

> Even though freediving is a one-person activity, it is recommended to have a dive buddy with you...When you have a friend with you, there is a sense of reassurance in you that there is this other person who can observe you.[5]

A free diver knows that the more air you can get into your lungs, the deeper you can dive beneath the surface of the water and the longer you can stay there. And the more we're filled with the fullness of God, the deeper we can dive into the knowledge of God, where we can explore the depths of his love and can drink from the ocean of his wisdom.

This fullness can also give us endurance, for God is "over all and through all and in all" (Ephesians 4:6). Furthermore, wisdom tells us that going it alone is never the way to go. First Peter 5:7 says you are to "cast all your anxieties on him because he cares for you."

It may be a challenge to believe, but the God who wants you to be like him and live for him really does want you to be filled with him. And I think that's so you can know the thrill of him. When you're full of God, he's right there with his presence and power, right there to observe and help you whenever you need him, right there to be evident to everyone you encounter throughout your day. And "out of his fullness," the disciple John wrote, you will also receive grace (John 1:6).

No, I don't know everything this particular part of Ephesians 3:19 means, but I mean it when I say I want to be filled with God's fullness.

> *God, may I be so full of your presence and power that anyone I encounter will sense the aroma of your fullness in my life. I ask you to fill me full, and then when I am, fill me to overflowing for the sake of others. In Jesus' name I pray, amen.*

MORE THAN ABLE

Prayer can do anything God can do—
and God can do anything![1]

ADRIAN ROGERS

didn't take up golf until I was in my forties, but as I mentioned in an earlier devotion, when I did, that bug bit me hard. And since then, I've been privileged to play some of the best golf courses in the world. From the outset, though, the one course I wanted to play above all others was the one at Augusta National Golf Club in Georgia.

For my fiftieth birthday, my wife wanted to surprise me with a chance to play on this amazing golf course, so she made a phone call. Over the years we'd come to know one of the most influential men in Georgia, and we considered him a very good friend. So Teresa called him to ask if he could get me on that golf course. Surprisingly, he said he had no connections whatsoever to help her.

Through a dear pastor friend of ours who knew a member at the club, Teresa did get me on that course. But I, too, was surprised the first man couldn't fulfill her request given his sphere of influence. (By the way, of all the courses I've played, I still believe Augusta National is the best.)

Years later, a woman who'd been that man's personal assistant visited me. During the course of our conversation, she brought up the phone call Teresa made to him. I had long forgotten about the incident, but she told me he'd been more than able to get me on that golf course and that a single phone call to any number of people he knew would have done it. He just simply refused to help—and lied! I won't go into the reasons she told me he did that, but frankly, the disappointment lingers to this day.

It's one thing to approach a friend who can open a door for you only to learn they truly can't. It's another thing altogether to approach a friend who can open a door for you but simply refuses to put their hand on the doorknob. All of which leads us to one of the most amazing things you will ever read about in the Bible—God's ability and his willingness to use it on our behalf.

Paul has concluded telling the church in Ephesus about this prayer for them, but then he reminds them who hears his prayers—and theirs. He writes, "Now to him who is able to do immeasurably more than all we ask or imagine" (Ephesians 3:20).

You might say we've now come to the end of the *theology* of his prayer and come to the *doxology* of his prayer. Although the word "doxology" isn't found in the Bible, doxologies themselves certainly are. Doxology comes from the Latin term *doxologia*, which comes from the Greek term *doxa* meaning "glory," and the suffix *logia*, which refers to "a word spoken." A doxology is a verbal "expression of praise to God."[2]

As James Montgomery Boice writes, the closing words in Ephesians 3:20 may be the greatest doxology in the entire Bible.[3] First, Paul wants to emphasize not just the God who hears and answers prayer, but the incomparable ability he has. He uses words that ensure no one misses his point: "immeasurably more than all we ask or imagine."

How seriously we take prayer and how seriously we pray are determined by whether we believe these words about God's ability. Too often we fail to focus on God's power, and that's why when we think about what we'll pray for and how we'll pray for it, we better remember to whom we'll be praying.

Nothing reveals more about what you really believe about God than what you really believe about prayer. If your theology of prayer is correct, it will always lead to a doxology that brings glory and honor to the One to whom you pray. Because if Paul's statement is true, then neither the most brilliant minds nor the most creative geniuses in the world can think or imagine anything greater than what God can do.

You might be thinking, *But I've prayed prayers God couldn't answer.* Let me correct you. You've never prayed a prayer that God couldn't answer. Even no is an answer, and never think God's denial is because your prayer exceeded his power. It's always because his plan exceeded your prayer. You're praying to a God who has no limits on what he knows and what he can do. Jesus said, "All things are possible with God" (Mark 10:27).

The true test of what you believe about God is not what you say but how you pray. Think about the faith you bring to your prayer life and how you truly pray, then consider this question: If other people listened only to your prayers, would they believe you really trust in a God who can do far more than we ask or imagine?

Yes, our God can do immeasurably more than what we ask with our mouth or even conceive in our mind. There's no problem he can't solve, no person he can't save, no purpose he can't fulfill, and certainly no prayer he can't answer.

Is God able to answer all prayer and any prayer? Yes. He's more than able! Even if his answer isn't *yes*—at least to what you thought you wanted—but *no* or even *wait*, God is listening, and he knows what he's doing. Mother Teresa said, "Prayer is putting oneself in the hands of God"[4]—just where we belong.

God, I'm so thankful you're more than able to do exceedingly and abundantly above all that I ask or imagine. May my prayers always honor your power and willingness to work out all things for those who love you. In Jesus' name, amen.

21

THE ENDGAME

A hostile alien army came charging through a hole in space. We're standing 300 feet below it. We're the Avengers. We can bust arms dealers all the livelong day, but that up there that's...that's the endgame.[1]

TONY STARK, AKA IRONMAN

I admit I'm an unabashed, unashamed Avengers fan, and Ironman is my favorite one.

In the 2015 action film *Avengers: Age of Ultron,* Ironman is facing an alien invasion of New York City, and the continuation of the human race is in the balance. At one point he—played by Robert Downey Jr. (one of my favorite actors)—unequivocally explains to his team that defeating the aliens is the "endgame."

The "endgame" is "the final stage of some process or action."[2] And this is a fitting word to describe how Paul ends his prison prayer in the third chapter of Ephesians. In the last part of the last sentence, he succinctly reveals the endgame not just of prayer, but of life, of history, and, in fact, of eternity. He writes to the church in Ephesus, "To him be glory in the church and in Christ Jesus throughout all generations, for ever and ever! Amen" (Ephesians 3:21). A person once said, "There are two great moments in a person's life. The first is when you were born and the second is when you discover why you were born."

It's no surprise that this is a question I've been asked many times, especially by teenagers: "Why did God create me?" It seems like a challenging question, so whoever's asking is almost always surprised by how quickly I answer, "To bring God glory."

You see, God created everyone who's ever existed for the same purpose: *the glory of God.* So in your mind you must settle this one fundamental thing about the human race, and the earlier the better: None of us was put on this earth for our gain; we were put on this earth for God's glory. And that will be true for anyone not yet born as well.

We can always petition God for what we need. First John 5:14 says, "We can ask anything according to his will, and he hears us." But prayer is not to *convince* God to do something for us; it's primarily to ask him to do something in us. And what God wants to do in us is bring himself glory. Every prayer we pray is to be to the glory of God. This hurts to say and hurts to hear, but if you think the endgame is persuading God to do your bidding, you shouldn't be surprised when the answer to your prayer is no.

Be honest. Have you ever wondered why God insists on being glorified? Max Anders gives an answer I think is right: "God calls on us to glorify Him because, for our good, He wants us to perceive His value. He wants us to understand that He is the ground, the source of all that is truly good, pleasing, joyous, beneficial, blessed."[3]

But what does "the glory of God" mean? The best dictionary definitions for the word "glory" in this context are "worshipful praise, honor, and thanksgiving" and "something that secures praise or renown."[4] And so when we say, "the glory of God," we're referring to the greatness, the grandeur, and the goodness of God.

Now, please understand that God doesn't just deserve glory; he *is* glory. He's the only being in all the universe who is glorious, who radiates glory.

He doesn't need us to give him glory because he already has it. So even if we don't praise God, exalt God, or give God glory, he's still glorious.

So then why are we to give him glory and recognize his glory and do all things for his glory? *Because he's God and he deserves it.* One commentary says, "When we glorify [God], we acknowledge His greatness and splendor and laud Him for it. When we 'give Him glory'…we direct our praise, adoration, thanksgiving, and worship to Him who alone is worthy."[5]

You don't add to God's glory when you give it, and when you don't give it, you don't take away from it. But to refuse to live for God and give him glory brings incredible damage to your life. You won't experience the real endgame. You'll never fulfill your genuine purpose in life. You'll never find lasting fulfillment and peace. None of this will happen until and unless you realize your one goal should always be to act to the glory of God in whatever you do, in wherever you go, and in whatever you say. Our major purpose in life is to walk, talk, and, yes, even to pray in such a way that we recognize his glory, exalt his glory, and seek his glory.

Have you ever noticed that when someone shows you a photo of a group you were in, the first person you look at is you? When you're deciding whether you like the picture, you don't necessarily consider how everyone else looks; you focus on how you look. Why? Because we're all born with a default setting that's self-centered. Deep down, we're all born thinking, *It's all about me.*

Except it isn't.

So a good way to end your prayers each day is not just with the word "amen," but with the words "No matter what you decide to do, Lord, do it all for your glory." And then you can truly say, "Amen."

Take this thought from author Mark Batterson with you today: "It's not about success or failure. It's not about good days and bad days. It's not about wealth and poverty. It's not about health or sickness. It's not even about life or death. It's about glorifying God in whatever circumstance you find yourself in."[6]

The endgame of even our prayer life should always be what Paul tells us in Ephesians 3:21 about God: "To him be glory." The God who hears deserves nothing less.

Glorious Father, take every request I make and every need I bring and answer in such a way that you are glorified now and forever. You deserve all the glory, now and forever. Amen.

PHILIPPIANS 1:9-11

This is my prayer: that your love may abound more and more in knowledge and depth of insight, so that you may be able to discern what is best and may be pure and blameless for the day of Christ, filled with the fruit of righteousness that comes through Jesus Christ—to the glory and praise of God.

22

GROWING UP

Spiritual maturity is not reached by the passing of the years,
but by obedience to the will of God.[1]

OSWALD CHAMBERS

E very child is asked this question too many times to count. Weren't you? Parents, grandparents, friends, teachers, and even strangers say, "What do you want to be when you grow up?" The question assumes the child will mature not only physically but also in other ways as well.

Growth and maturity are vitally important to every aspect of your life. It's why we measure maturity in so many ways. We measure *physical maturity*—for example, as we age, we measure how much taller we have grown and how much weight we have gained. (In fact, one mark of maturity is when you finally realize you keep getting heavier without getting taller.)

We measure *intellectual maturity*—we require entrance exams into schools and final exams at the end of semesters and IQ tests because many jobs and vocations require a certain level of intellectual maturity to be successful.

We measure *emotional maturity*—the term used today is "emotional intelligence." EQ is the measurement of your ability to manage yourself in relationships, your career, and your life in a proper fashion. It is recognized as a key component in leadership ability.

Our heavenly Father expects us to mature spiritually as well. When we come into his family, we're just spiritual babies, but he doesn't want us to reach heaven as spiritually immature as we were the day we accepted Jesus. He wants us to grow in maturity while we still live on Earth.

If this next prayer of Paul's has one central, unifying theme, it's spiritual maturity.

> This is my prayer: that your love may abound more and more in knowledge and depth of insight, so that you may be able to discern what is best and may be pure and blameless for the day of Christ, filled with the fruit of righteousness that comes through Jesus Christ—to the glory and praise of God (Philippians 1:9-11).

You can see this prayer is centered around the Philippian Christians growing in relationship with the Lord and becoming more and more spiritually mature. But praying for growth and maturity may be more challenging than we think. Peter encouraged believers to mature spiritually when he said, "Make every effort to add to your faith goodness; and to goodness, knowledge; and to knowledge, self-control; and to self-control, perseverance; and to perseverance, godliness; and to godliness, mutual affection; and to mutual affection, love" (2 Peter 1:5-7).

Here's an observation from authors Kent Carlson and Mike Lueken in their book *Renovation of the Church*. They're talking about transformation, but I think what they have to say applies to the topic of seeking spiritual maturity as well.

> Paul wanted [the Philippians] to grow toward fullness in Christ. We nod in agreement with Paul's words. We like his words...But at the end of the day, a good percentage of us really don't want to experience the reality depicted by these words. We like our lives just fine. They may need a touch up here or there, but nothing too radical, nothing too extreme.

We'd be better off if we just admitted it. It is sufficient for us that Jesus has forgiven our sins and secured our eternity, leaving our daily lives relatively unaffected. We are the self-absorbed spouses we have always been. We continue to have a miser's heart. We use anger to overwhelm our opponents. We are trapped in lust. We manipulate and control to get what we want. We trust our political party more than Jesus. We ignore the poor. We have personal policies that are categorically opposed to the teaching of Christ. But we aren't bothered enough by these disconnects to put forth the effort to cooperate with the Holy Spirit because, in spite of what we claim, we really don't believe transformation is that important.[2]

How do we know we're spiritually maturing? In this list of six ways we can tell, the author of this list uses the words "marked by."

1. We're marked by abounding love.
2. We're marked by growing knowledge.
3. We're marked by spiritual discernment.
4. We're marked by spiritual integrity.
5. We're marked by good works.
6. We're marked by glorifying God.[3]

Keep these things in mind as we begin our study of this next prison prayer found in the book of Philippians. If this prayer has one central unifying theme, it would be that of spiritual maturity. One of the greatest indicators of spiritual maturity in your life—and whether or not you are continuing to mature—is your prayer life. In fact, stop right now and ask yourself this question: Would the content, the level, and the direction of my prayers be more like that of a baby, a toddler, a child, or an adult?

The first time I really felt that I was growing up and approaching adulthood was when I began driving a car. Toddlers ride in strollers and kids ride bikes (although adults still do), but only those who have reached a certain level of maturity are allowed to drive cars. That leads to a very interesting observation author Larry Crabb made about the prayer life of many Christians.

> Look around your church and look at yourself in the mirror. Talk to other people about their prayer life and think about your own. You may come to this conclusion—that the church, especially the evangelical church, is filled with big kids riding in strollers or bikes when they ought to be driving cars in the way they pray.[4]

I believe the bottom line is this: "Spiritual maturity is achieved through becoming more like Jesus Christ."[5] And in seeing how the apostle prayed for the Philippians, we're given an indicator of whether we're becoming more like Christ—whether we're more like him in our prayer lives.

Of course, there's no such thing as instant maturity. As author Steve Farrar wrote, a lot of things can be instant, like instant oatmeal, instant coffee, instant soup, and microwave popcorn. But you can't hurry spiritual maturity. In fact, he said, the process is more like God putting us in a slow cooker![6]

In our study of this prayer part by part, I pray you're ready to become more and more like Jesus—spiritually mature.

Father, thank you for hearing me when I come to you as one of your children. And though I want to have a childlike faith, I never want to remain childish in the way I live out my faith. Transform me into a more spiritually mature person, and may my prayer life reflect the growth taking place. In Jesus' name, amen.

23

THE LOVE OF YOUR LIFE

Love is the beauty of the soul.[1]
SAINT AUGUSTINE

n telling the church in Philippi about his prayer for them, Paul begins by focusing on the foundation of and one of the fruits of true spiritual maturity—love. He writes, "This is my prayer: that your love may abound more and more in knowledge and depth of insight" (Philippians 1:9). We need to ask God not only for a love that shows but a love that grows—a love that will abound more and more.

Real love never remains the same in either quality or quantity, for it's one thing to possess love but another to progress in love. We begin with our love for God, the one we should love the most because he's the one who loves us the most. But then our love should grow wider, meaning we should love more people. We are to love our parents, our children, other family members, our neighbors, our friends—even our enemies (Matthew 5:4; Luke 6:28, 35).

Yet our love should also grow deeper, meaning we should love people more. We need to pray for a love that even flows out of us. In fact, we should pray for a love that overflows! If you pour a carbonated drink into a glass of ice too quickly, fizz will explode to the top of the glass and overflow. Our love for God, the church, our family, our friends, our neighbors, and, yes, even our enemies should overflow like exploding fizz. It should abound.

I've been married to my wife for many years, and my love for her is deeper, wider, fuller, bigger, and stronger than it's ever been. I loved Teresa on our wedding day, but to compare the love I have for her now to the love I had for her decades ago would be like comparing the sun to a flashlight.

The love Paul's talking about is *agape* love—a divine love. It's a godlike love, and it's more than an emotion. It's an action. C.S. Lewis put it brilliantly when he said this:

> It would be quite wrong to think that the way to become loving is to sit trying to manufacture affectionate feelings…The rules for all of us is perfectly simple. Do not waste time bothering whether you "love" your neighbor. Act as if you did. When we do this, we find one of the great secrets. When you are behaving as if you love someone you will presently come to love him.[2]

As Paul did on behalf of the Philippians, we should ask God to give us this mature love that will not only abound more and more but "in knowledge and depth of insight." How does love grow in knowledge? In the Bible, the word "knowledge" almost always refers to the knowledge of God. Remember what Peter said? "Make every effort to add to your faith goodness; and to goodness, *knowledge*" (2 Peter 1:5). True love always comes from God, and the more you know him, the better you will love him and the better you will love others the way he loves them.

But true love is not blind. True love knows. True love discerns. And true love acts. So when you see someone on a wrong path, taking them away from God, love them enough to show them the right path and how to get there. But you're responsible to do this the right way—with love—not only for the sake of the other person but for your sake as well. Remember, Paul said, "Speaking the truth in love, we will grow to become in every respect the mature body of him who is the head, that is, Christ" (Ephesians 4:15).

Be warned, however. Loving someone doesn't mean they will love you back. Yet mature love doesn't give love to receive it; it gives love expecting nothing in return. And this is true even when we don't feel love toward someone. Someone defined love as "a feeling unlike any feeling you have ever felt before." But love is not a feeling. It is an action, something you will do whether you feel like it or not.

Last, mature love has "depth of insight." That refers to discernment. It's one thing to know whom to love; it's another to know how to love them and to love them in the best way. True love always does what's best for the other person. Yes, we are required to love everybody, but we are responsible to love them the right way. Love is not blind. True love sees. True love knows. True love discerns. True love acts.

This, then, should be the love of your life and the love with which you pray to the God who hears for the people in your life—*agape* love.

Father, I know I am to love because you are love. I admit I don't always love as I should, but may my love grow wider and deeper. May I love more people and love people more, knowing and discerning that the best way to do that is to first love you with all of my heart. In Jesus' name I pray, amen.

24

THE BEST CHOICE

The choice to make good choices is the best choice you can choose.
Fail to make that choice and on most choices you will lose.[1]

RYAN LILLY

One of the greatest gifts God has given us is the freedom to make choices. But with that gift comes responsibility and accountability. We have the responsibility to make wise choices, but we're accountable even when we don't. We're not free from the consequences of our choices, good or bad. They're like boomerangs. In some form or another, they always come back to us.

That's why the next part of Paul's letter to the church in Philippi is so vital to the Christian life. His prayer was that their "love may abound more and more in knowledge and depth of insight" with the purpose that they would "be able to discern what is best" (Philippians 1:9-10).

"Depth of insight" calls for something money can't buy, thieves can't steal, and can't be borrowed from someone else—discernment. Discernment calls for both examination and evaluation, so every decision involves both examining the choices before us and evaluating them to determine what the best choice would be.

Rarely is the biggest challenge we face in making decisions trying to discern between what's good and what's bad. That's usually easy. The real challenge is discerning between what's good and what's best. As one Bible commentary says, the word "best" used in Philippians 1:10 refers not to things that differ but things that excel, things that can surpass everything else compared to it.[2]

Sometimes choices are a matter of patience, because far too often people settle for what's good instead of waiting for what's best. But our heavenly Father is just like an earthly father. He wants what's best for his children, and sometimes that means we must wait. I learned this lesson personally, and I thank God that I did.

While pastoring a church in Mississippi, I experienced a burning desire to get back to my home state of Georgia. The pastorate position where I'd served as a youth pastor opened up, and I just knew they were going to call me because I was so sure this was the church for me. But I never heard from them, and my disappointment was palpable.

Soon after that, another church position opened up in Atlanta, and they did call me. The church I thought I wanted was and is a good church, but I now know the church I moved to instead was the best one for me.

You see, good is better than bad, but best is better than good. And God always wants what's best for us, not just what's good.

My pastoring mentor and preaching model was the late Dr. Adrian Rogers. When I had the privilege of spending almost an entire day with him, we discussed building a personal library.

"James," he said, "so often people ask me, 'Have you read any good books lately?'" Then he smiled and said, "It shocks them when I say, 'No, I haven't. In fact, I never read good books.' I pause for a dramatic moment and then say, 'You see, I don't have time to read good books. I try to read only the best books.'" Then he advised me to always make sure to stock my library with the best books.

We desperately need to ask the Holy Spirit to help us discern what's best. How much happier would some people be today if they'd asked for discernment to determine the best person to marry, the best way to manage their money, the best friends to choose, the best way to do a job, the best way to raise children, or the best way to live. Today, more than ever, parents need to ask God to help their children learn to discern not just what's right and what's wrong, what's true and what's false, and what's good and what's evil, but what's best.

Just a little discernment can make the difference between an agonizing defeat and a tremendous victory. When Tiger Woods used Nike golf equipment, the company sent him five prototype drivers to try. He practiced with each one and then told them he thought the best driver, his favorite, was the one that weighed the most.

Nike's club makers were completely baffled because they believed all five clubs weighed exactly the same. But they put each one on a scale, and to their amazement they discovered that Woods' favorite club was the heaviest—*by less than an ounce.*[3] If Woods is that discerning about a driver, how much more discerning should we be in what we see, hear, believe, and live.

Is there any greater need in the church today than spiritual discernment? As Charles R. Swindoll said, we need it in "what we see and what we hear and what we believe."[4] Thank God he's listening when we pray.

Father of all wisdom, I need discernment in every decision I make. I want to choose only what's best, because I know that's what you want for my life. May I show my growing love for you by displaying a discernment that always chooses your best for me. In Jesus' name. Amen.

PASS WITH FLYING COLORS

Live in such a way that you would not be ashamed
to sell your parrot to the biggest gossip in town.[1]

WILL ROGERS

The more I pray as Paul did in this Philippians 1 prayer, the more I understand that if the love of God abounds in my heart and I love him and others the way I should, I'm motivated to live a life of praying for discernment and making the best choices. If we all do that, the result will be that we are "pure and blameless for the day of Christ" (Philippians 1:10).

Using the NIV, "the day of Christ" or "the day of Lord Jesus" appears several times in the New Testament. Paul also uses one of those phrases in Philippians 1:6, Philippians 2:16, and 1 Corinthians 1:8. The term refers to the end of the world—when Christ returns.

Let's break down what the two key words in this passage—"pure" and "blameless"—mean.

The word "pure" is used multiple times in the New Testament. Here, it's a combination of two Greek words that mean "to judge" and "to judge by sunlight."[2] The word is translated elsewhere as "sincere," which is a good word in this passage because honest dealers in the world of pottery found it necessary to mark their product with the Latin *sine cera*, meaning "without wax" and often translated "sincere."

> In New Testament times, the finest and most expensive pottery was thin and clear in color. Its thinness made it very fragile. During the firing process, this pottery would often crack in the oven. But dishonest dealers did not throw away their cracked pottery. Instead, they filled the cracks with a hard, pearly wax, one that would easily blend in with the color of the pottery. The cracks became virtually invisible...Those who were aware and wary of unscrupulous pottery dealers knew that the wax was immediately detectable if the pottery were held up to the light, especially to sunlight.[3]

In other words, to be "pure" means to be "the real deal," that you are in private what you are in public. No one is sure who said this in a humorous fashion, but someone did, and it's the truth: Be who you is, because if you is who you ain't, you ain't who you is.

Paul also prayed that the church at Philippi would be blameless. Blameless means walking in the ways of the Lord. Blameless is someone who "does what is righteous, who speaks the truth from their heart; whose tongue utters no slander, who does no wrong to a neighbor, and casts no slur on others" (Psalm 15:2-3). We not only want to be blameless on the day of Christ, but also here and now.

One thing blameless means is not causing someone else to sin. In his letter to the Romans, Paul wrote, "Make up your mind not to put any stumbling block or obstacle in the way of a brother or sister" (Romans 14:13). We all have influence over other people, but our lives should never be a barrier to someone coming to Christ; they should be a bridge to their coming to Christ. People may stumble, but if so, it should be over their own sins, not ours.

I'm not suggesting trying to be perfect. None of us will ever be perfect this side of heaven, but we can be and should be blameless. So before you do or say anything you're not sure about, ask yourself these three questions:

1. Would this make someone else fail, falter, or fall?

2. Would this make Christ ashamed of me?

3. Would this make me guilty before God?

Theologian Jonathan Edwards made many resolutions like this one: "Resolved, never to do anything which I should be afraid to do if it were the last hour of my life."[4] I would add to that, especially if that last hour is the hour when Jesus Christ returns.

Commenting on how Paul showed himself certain that God works in the lives of his people to make them blameless, John Piper shares these verses from letters the apostle wrote to the Thessalonians and Corinthians and to the Philippians earlier in his letter to them:

> May your whole spirit, soul and body be kept blameless at the coming of our Lord Jesus Christ. The one who calls you is faithful, and he will do it (1 Thessalonians 5:23-24).

> He will also keep you firm to the end, so that you will be blameless on the day of our Lord Jesus Christ (1 Corinthians 1:8).

> He who began a good work in you will carry it on to completion until the day of Christ Jesus (Philippians 1:6).

Then Piper adds, "Paul does not simply watch this dynamic play out in the lives of his converts. He prays for them."[5] Likewise, we can and should pray not just for ourselves but for others, asking that they, too, will be found pure and blameless before the Lord.

As ships returned from war back in the day, their flags were raised or lowered to signify whether they'd been victorious or defeated. When the flags flew high, they "passed with flying colors."[6] Today might be the last day of your life or the day of Christ's return, but either way, may you be found pure and blameless, having passed the test with flying colors.

God, I don't know what I'll face today or who I'll deal with, but with every test and temptation I face, make me pure and blameless so I will pass with flying colors. In the name of the God who hears, amen.

HIGH-HANGING FRUIT

Don't shine so others can see you.
Shine so that through you others can see Him.[1]

C.S. LEWIS

magine you're alone with God, entering his presence, and you start right in with presenting a laundry list of your needs you want him to meet, your desires you want him to fulfill, and whatever you want him to give you. But what if instead you began this prayer time by asking, *Lord, what do you want from me? What do you want to do through me?* I believe God would simply answer, *Fruit. I want to bear fruit through you.*

Paul concludes his prayer for the church by asking that they be "filled with the fruit of righteousness that comes through Jesus Christ—to the glory and praise of God" (Philippians 1:11). Let's look at what a couple of commentaries tell us:

- In the natural world, fruit is the result of a healthy plant producing what it was designed to produce (Genesis 1:11-12). In the Bible, the word *fruit* is often used to describe a person's outward actions that result from the condition of the heart.[2]

- Dictionaries define *righteousness* as 'behavior that is morally justifi-
able or right.' Such behavior is characterized by accepted standards
of morality, justice, virtue, or uprightness. The Bible's standard of
human righteousness is God's own perfection in every attribute,
every attitude, every behavior, and every word.[3]

But what is the key to bearing this fruit? Any farmer or viticulturist will
tell you the key to bearing physical fruit is the plant or vine's root. The most
beautiful branch coming from any fruit-bearing tree or vine may have the
greenest leaves you can imagine, but if the branch is severed from the tree or
vine itself, and therefore from the root, that branch will never bear fruit. The
root bears the fruit through the branch.

This is why Paul refers to this fruit of righteousness as that which "comes
through Jesus Christ." And note this carefully: Righteousness is not what
you do for God; it's what God does through you. We are not to show Jesus
what we can do for him; we are to show others what Jesus can do through us
and therefore through them. When you see apples on a tree, you know they
didn't produce the tree. The tree produced the apples.

Here's how we know when righteousness is from God, not from human
effort:

- *The glory goes to God.* True righteousness originates with God, not
with us. True righteousness elevates God, not us. If righteousness
comes from us, we will take the glory. But if righteousness comes
from God, he gets the glory.

- *Our fruit is acceptable to God.* Only a life that finds its root in a relationship with Jesus Christ bears fruit that God accepts. No one will
ever have righteousness before God until they're right with him, and

they will never be right with God until they surrender their life to the most righteous person who ever lived—Jesus Christ.

- *We are perfect in God's sight.* Max Lucado observed, "In the Chinese language the word for *righteousness* is a combination of two characters, the figure of a lamb and a person. The lamb is on top, covering the person. Whenever God looks down at you, this is what he sees: the perfect Lamb of God covering you."[4]

This is why a vital prayer life is so important and the power of prayer can never be underestimated. Only through praying do we renew, revitalize, and reawaken the connection to the only root that bears real fruit—the God who hears. We devote so much of our praying to nearly everything except what we should pray about, but more than ever I'm convinced that if, every day, we simply ask God to fill us with the fruit of the righteousness that comes only through Jesus, he will take care of everything else.

Then Paul adds, "to the glory and praise of God." This is what every life rightly lived should be for. "God's ultimate goal is to uphold and display the glory of his name."[5] And that is the ultimate goal of the Christian life. How is this done? Through bearing fruit. Bearing fruit and glorifying God are organically linked together. Jesus said to his disciples, "I chose you and appointed you so that you might go and bear fruit" (John 15:16). He also said, "This is to my Father's glory, that you bear much fruit, showing yourselves to be my disciples" (verse 8).

One way we glorify God is by serving him, through which he can produce fruit. Charles Spurgeon said, "How can you serve the Lord with your lips if you do not serve Him with your lives?"[6]

Simply put, the God-glorifying Christian is the fruit-bearing Christian.

Father, as I stay connected to the root of Jesus Christ, your Son, bear through me real fruit and real righteousness that bring you glory. May others in my life see not what I'm doing for you but what you're doing for and in me and what you can do for and in them. In Jesus' name, amen.

COLOSSIANS 1:9-14

Since the day we heard about you, we have not stopped praying for you. We continually ask God to fill you with the knowledge of his will through all the wisdom and understanding that the Spirit gives, so that you may live a life worthy of the Lord and please him in every way: bearing fruit in every good work, growing in the knowledge of God, being strengthened with all power according to his glorious might so that you may have great endurance and patience, and giving joyful thanks to the Father, who has qualified you to share in the inheritance of his holy people in the kingdom of light. For he has rescued us from the dominion of darkness and brought us into the kingdom of the Son he loves, in whom we have redemption, the forgiveness of sins.

NO WASTED TIME

Pray in the Spirit on all occasions with all kinds of prayers.

EPHESIANS 6:18

aul's letter to the Colossians is unique among the four we're exploring not only because it's the shortest, but also because he was writing to a church he hadn't founded or even visited. He'd never met one single Christian in Colossae. Yet he prayed what I believe is a perfect prayer for any church and any people.

You probably know the Latin phrase *carpe diem*, which means "seize the day." Well, I call this a *carpe diem* prayer because you won't find a prayer that can do more in us, for us, with us, and ultimately through us than this one of Paul's. Furthermore, we can pray it personalized and confidently, assured that God will not only hear it but agree with it and answer it. And as Billy Graham said, "You can pray anytime, anywhere. Washing dishes, digging ditches, working in the office, in the shop, on the athletic field, even in prison—you can pray and know God hears!"[1]

The prayer Jesus gave as a model prayer in Matthew 6:9-13, known as the Lord's Prayer, is only 53 words long, and I've noticed something similar about all four of these prison prayers. As Paul presents them, they're surprisingly brief. Using the New International Version of the Bible, I counted the words in each passage and then read them out loud. Here are my results:

- Ephesians 1:15-23 (198 words, 48 seconds)

- Ephesians 3:14-21 (154 words, 41 seconds)

- Philippians 1:9-11 (59 words, 17 seconds)

- Colossians 1:9-14 (143 words, 35 seconds)

We can pray all kinds of prayers on all kinds of occasions and of all kinds of lengths, including brief prayers. Sometimes short prayers are the best, getting right to the point with the Lord. And it's important not to lengthen prayers for no good reason, especially with empty words. Jesus said, "When you pray, do not keep on babbling like pagans, for they think they will be heard because of their many words. Do not be like them, for your Father knows what you need before you ask him" (Matthew 6:7-8).

Paul certainly didn't babble as he wrote to these churches. No doubt these prayers are short and brief, but who would deny that they are deep and powerful? I call your attention to this because I want to impress upon you that often in life and in prayer, depth, not length, is important.

And who would deny these prayers' depth and power? As Charles Swindoll shared in one of his books, history has a profound example of brevity that counts:

> When the Gettysburg battleground became a national cemetery, Edward Everett was to give the dedication speech and Abraham Lincoln asked to say "a few appropriate words." Everett spoke

eloquently for one hour and fifty-seven minutes then took his seat as the crowd roared its enthusiastic approval. Then Lincoln stood to his feet, slipped on his steel spectacles, and began what we know today as the "Gettysburg Address." Poignant words "…The world will little note nor long remember…"—suddenly, he was finished. No more than two minutes after he had begun, he stopped. His talk had been so prayerlike it seemed almost inappropriate to applaud.

As Lincoln sank into his settee, John Young of the *Philadelphia Press* whispered, "Is that all?" The president answered, "Yes, that's all." Shortly after that Everett wrote a letter to the president commending the "eloquent simplicity & appropriateness" of his remarks. Everett went on to say, "I should be glad, if I could flatter myself that I came as near to the central idea of the occasion, in two hours, as you did in two minutes."

Swindoll concluded with, "Don't underestimate two minutes with God in prayer."[2]

Always remember that you may pray to the God who hears you not only anytime but as often as you need and in as short or long a manner as seems right for your current situation or in relation to what you're praying about.

Not long ago, I came across this statement:

> You can tell what a person likes by what they do.
> You can tell what a person thinks by what they say,
> but you can tell what a person is by how they pray.

I believe that is true if you think about it because what else measures a person more than how they talk to God?

As we continue our journey, remember that the length of your prayers doesn't matter, nor where or how often they are prayed throughout your day or whether they are presented in words or with a groan. As long as they're deep and intimate, you are never wasting time.

Father, thank you for granting me the privilege of coming to you in prayer each day and throughout the day. I know that whether my prayers are short or long or even a groan, their depth is what counts to you. You hear, answer, and comfort, and I'm so grateful for that. In Jesus' name, amen.

NO HARD STOPS

The value of persistent prayer is not that God will hear us,
but that we will finally hear God.[1]

WILLIAM MCGILL

At a recent question and answer session at our church, someone asked a question I'd never been asked during my many years of ministry: "When should I stop praying about something?" I admit I really had to give this query some thought. It's a hard and yet fair question. After all, I'm sure we've all been tempted to stop praying about something. In fact, most of us *have* stopped at one time or another.

Yet John Piper suggests one reason a hard stop on a prayer shouldn't be an option for us:

> Isn't it significant (I think it is) that in the Bible we have the statement "You do not have because you do not ask" (James 4:2), but we don't have the statement "You pray too much or too long"? We don't have a statement that says, "You have things I did not want to give you because you kept on asking me when it was time to quit." We don't have anything like that.[2]

This leads us to how Paul begins this prison prayer to the Colossians. He says, "Since the day we heard about you, we have not stopped praying for you. We continually ask God…" (Colossians 1:9). Paul made basically this same declaration in the first prayer we studied in Ephesians, that time using the personal pronoun "I" rather than including the people with whom he did ministry in "we." He said in Ephesians chapter 1, "I have not stopped giving thanks for you, remembering you in my prayers. I keep asking…" (verses 16-17).

Paul wasn't just a prayer; he was a persistent prayer. When it came to prayer, he didn't know the meaning of the word quit.

I'm a history buff, particularly interested in American history. One branch of history that holds a lot of fascination for me is what is called "Counterfactual Theory." Counterfactual theorists ask what-if questions. For example, *What if the United States had lost the Revolutionary War?* or *What if Germany had gotten the atomic bomb first?*

Here's a Bible alternate history from author Mark Batterson: "What if the Israelites had stopped circling [Jericho] on the sixth day? The answer is obvious. They would have forfeited the miracle right before it happened." Humorously, he adds, "They would have done a lot of walking for nothing." And then he perfectly states what the problem is today: "Our generation desperately needs to rediscover the difference between praying for and praying through."[3] And praying through means not stopping.

Pepsi scored a big hit with their 2008 Super Bowl ad, "Which House Is Bob's?" where two deaf actors use only sign language and captioning is provided for the hearing audience. It's based on a popular story in the deaf community that goes like this: "Two guys are driving to their friend Bob's house to watch the Super Bowl. Once they get to Bob's street, neither knows which house is his. They sit in the car, arguing, until one of them has an idea. He starts laying on the horn, and one by one, the houses light up and dogs start barking. One house stays dark and quiet: It's Bob's."[4] Because the two men kept honking, they accomplished their mission and found what they were looking for.

Sometimes we're convinced we're praying in the will of God, praying for something that's right and good, and the answer we seek doesn't come. We're discouraged. But the problem is that the devil has put a stop sign in front of our heart, trying to get us to quit doing the one thing he probably fears more than anything else—praying. Pastor Jim Cymbala said, "Persistent calling upon the name of the Lord breaks through every stronghold of the devil."[5]

Jesus, the greatest man of prayer who ever lived, told his disciples a parable about a widow who kept nagging a judge about giving her justice against someone who had wronged her. In telling us about this incident, Gospel writer Luke specifically mentions the point of Jesus' telling this story to his disciples: "to show them that they should always pray and not give up" (Luke 18:1). In Ephesians 6:18, Paul wrote, "Be alert and always keep on praying for all the Lord's people," and in Romans 12:12 he told the Romans to be "faithful in prayer."

The benefits of persistent prayer are important to recognize, and blogger Mark Altrogge shared these four:

1. It keeps us from treating God like a magical genie who grants all our wishes.

2. It causes us to depend on God, trusting him to give us what we need at just the right time.

3. It brings glory to God when he powerfully answers our prayers in unexpected ways.

4. It causes us to regularly draw near to God.[6]

I think we should be getting the point by now, don't you? We should never stop praying, not in general and not for any specific need. The God who hears expects to hear from us so we can hear from him. No hard stops!

Yes, there are times when we get discouraged in our prayer life. There are times we are convinced we are praying in the will of God, praying for something that is right and good, but the answer still doesn't come. Only the devil will put a stop sign in front of your heart to get you to quit doing the one thing he probably fears more than anything, and that is praying. With persistent prayer, you *will* at some point hear from God. One way or another, he always answers. So stay alert, be faithful, run that stop sign, and just keep blowing that prayer horn.

Father, I admit that sometimes a stop sign has appeared in front of my heart when it comes to prayer and I've actually stopped praying. Help me realize that's when I need to run the stop sign and continue to blow the horn of prayer. No hard stops! In Jesus' name I pray, amen.

THE HYPHEN

There is no substitute for the confidence that today—
in this time and place—I am obeying the will of my Father.[1]

CHARLES E. HUMMEL

When you walk through a cemetery or graveyard, you no doubt see the date of the deceased people's birth and the date of their death on the headstones or plaques. But what's between those two dates is rarely noticed—a short horizontal line, a hyphen.

Those hyphens represent individuals' entire lives. Their full stay on earth—whether long or short, happy or tragic, good or bad, glorious or shameful—is there. That's the real story of anyone's life.

As you read these words, traveling along that hyphen between your birth and your death, ask yourself this question: *Does that hyphen represent God's will or mine?* You can choose what your hyphen represents—either living out the will of this world or living out the will of the God who created it.

As we dive deeper into how Paul prayed for the church in Colossae, we find the linchpin that holds all the rest of his prayer together. He wrote, "We continually ask God to fill you with the knowledge of his will" (Colossians 1:9).

Compared to the other prison prayers we've studied, this one has a sequence. I would call it a perfect daily sequence because there's no better way to begin each day than by asking God to fill us with the knowledge of his will for the next 16 hours or so. There's no greater benefit than knowing that because we're living in the will of God, our Christian life will fall into place.

In the New Testament, to be filled means to be "controlled by." If you're filled with alcohol, you'll be controlled by its effects. If you're filled with hunger, you'll be controlled by your appetite. If you're filled with anger, you'll be controlled by your temper. To be filled with the knowledge of God's will, however, is to be controlled by his will.

Understand that the will of God Paul's talking about is not the will we so often go looking for. This isn't about questions like *Is it God's will for me to take this job?* or *Is it God's will for me to move to that city?* or *Is it God's will for me to marry this person?* John Piper teaches about the two wills of God: his sovereign will—"his control of all things"—and his will of command—"the will of God we can disobey and fail to do."[2] Here, Paul is talking about God's sovereign will.

But let's move to God's "will of command" for a minute. As a pastor, I don't think I've been asked any question more than *How can I know the will of God for my life?* And usually the people asking want to know his will about specific life choices. After all, "We are God's handiwork, created in Christ Jesus to do good works, which God prepared in advance for us to do" (Ephesians 2:10).

The first thing I do is affirm this truth: God wants us to know his will for us. He doesn't play cat-and-mouse or hide-and-seek or ask us to guess what's behind door number three. God is more eager for us to know his will for our lives than we are to find it! He's eager for us to understand his will, what it is, and then do it.

But here's something we need to remember: *You will never know the will of God that you don't yet know until you are willing to obey the will of God that you do know.* Think about it. Why would God reveal to you his will that you don't know if you are not going to obey his will that you do know?

King David wrote, "Teach me to do your will" (Psalm 143:10). He didn't say, "Lord, help me *find* your will." He said, "Lord, teach me to *do* your will." So that's the beginning. If you're struggling with finding the will of God for your life, ask yourself if you're obeying the will of God you already know. If you aren't, take a good hard look at your Christian walk. But if you are, feel free to seek God's will you don't yet know, no matter what that might be. It just has to be all about God's will, not yours.

How do we seek his will? Pray. Read God's Word. Mark Batterson says, "Prayer isn't about outlining our agenda to God; it's about getting into God's presence and getting God's agenda for us. If you don't know where to start, or if you get stuck, go back to the Bible. Start reading, and God will start speaking."[3]

Remember, every day lived between birth and death is all about that hyphen. And for Christians, it's about living according to God's will rather than according to the will of the world. The world's will steer you wrong; God's will never will. Psalm 3:5-6 should be embraced for this very reason. It says, "In all your ways submit to him, and he will make your paths straight."

Pastor George W. Truett said, "To know the will of God is the greatest knowledge! To do the will of God is the greatest achievement."[4] So ask God for his power to follow his will, the will you know. And when you're living a life of obedience to that will, then pray for God's will according to his purposes. John 9:31 says the Lord "listens to the godly person who does his will."

God, fill me with the knowledge of your will and the strength and desire to obey your will already revealed to me through prayer and your Word. Only then will I be ready to receive knowledge of your will I don't yet know. In Jesus' name, amen.

WHAT SHOULD YOU DO?

Knowledge comes from looking around;
wisdom comes from looking up.[1]

ADRIAN ROGERS

What should I do? is a popular question! There are more than 64 million Google results for the question, "What Should I Do?" People from all walks of life are now making a living by becoming what is known as "Advice Experts." *Time* magazine states,

> What was once an artform largely confined to syndicated newspaper columns is now a thriving industry, spanning not only written Q&As, but also live chats, apps, videos and audio…We have entered a new golden age of advice.[2]

There are all kinds of advice on the internet, and a lot of it is for free.

The Bible is clear that seeking counsel and advice from other people is wise, but with one caveat: We should make sure our advisors are wise, because even those considered "expert" and "legitimate" might not be wise. They might just know things.

Too many people find knowledgeable advice but not wise advice. As was mentioned in an earlier devotion, knowledge can tell you what you *can* do, but only wisdom can tell you what you *should* do. And this is why the next part of Paul's prayer on behalf of the Colossians makes so much sense. He prays for the church to be filled with the knowledge of God's will "through all the wisdom and understanding that the Spirit gives" (Colossians 1:9).

Wisdom can save so much heartache—especially when it comes to God's "will of command" we talked about in the last devotion. Even when we know the will of God in what we should do in specific situations or for specific life choices, we also need to know the right way to do it, the right time to do it, and the right place to do it. And this wisdom comes only through the wisdom and understanding we gain from God's Spirit.

Today we're living in a world that's floating in an ocean of knowledge yet dying in a desert of wisdom. You can gain knowledge from a book, but you can gain wisdom and understanding only from God-breathed Scripture and prayer. Unlike the world, God is more concerned about our SQ than our IQ—our *spiritual quotient* more than our *intellectual quotient*. A spoonful of godly wisdom and understanding is better than a bucket full of worldly knowledge when you need to make a decision. And knowledge without wisdom isn't just deficient. It can be dangerous and even destructive.

For example, today kids know more about sex at an earlier age than ever before, but that doesn't mean they have wisdom about it. They're getting *knowledgeable advice* on what to do and how to do it from places like public schools or books or videos their parents buy them, but they're not necessarily getting *wise advice* on when to do it, why to do it, and with whom to do it.

Here's the bottom line: When you have the God-given understanding that his will is best and the God-given wisdom only he can give, you won't have to find the will of God; the will of God will find you. God is eager to show his will to those who are wise enough to choose it and understand enough to apply it.

You may be in a situation right now where you're not exactly sure what you should do. May I humbly give you two pieces of advice?

First, don't fail to read and study the Word of God. This is where you'll find his general will, his sovereign will. As you look at your options for what to do, make sure they all fall within the boundaries of the truth found in the Bible. This alone will narrow your options.

Second, never fail to go to the God of the Word. The giver of all wisdom is willing, waiting, and wanting to give you the wisdom and understanding you need to know what his specific will is in any situation. Don't try to make a challenging decision without him. He's not only the God who hears, but also the God who answers, and he is always as specific as he needs to be. David of the Bible said to his Lord, "I call on you, my God, for you will answer me; turn your ear to me and hear my prayer" (Psalm 17:6).

In his book *Draw the Circle*, Mark Batterson writes,

> I love the story about the grandfather who walked by his granddaughter's bedroom one night and overheard her praying the alphabet, literally. "Dear God, a, b, c, d, e, f, g." She prayed all the way to "z" and said, "Amen." The grandfather said, "Sweetie, why were you praying that way?" The granddaughter replied, "I didn't know what to say so I figured I'd let God put the letters together however He saw fit."[3]

In every part of your life, God wants to put the letters together however he sees fit. When you don't know what to do, ask him to fill you with the knowledge of his will through the wisdom and understanding only he can give. You can rest assured he will.

Father, I'm so often in a situation where I need to know what to do and how to do it. When that happens, I will ask you to fill me with the knowledge of your will and give me the wisdom to discern it and the understanding to apply it, knowing I can leave the results to you. Amen.

31

WALK THE TALK

We should live in such a way that our lives
wouldn't make much sense if the gospel were not true.[1]

DOROTHY DAY

Not long after children are born, their families embrace a growing anticipation for a magical moment that happens in homes and hamlets every day and all over the world. And when that moment comes, grandparents make a video, parents post the news along with photos all over social media, and older siblings might even love it. Joy explodes everywhere!

This is the moment babies take their first step. They put one foot in front of the other and start walking. You've probably heard this proverb from ancient China: A journey of a thousand miles begins with a single step. Here's another saying, its origin unknown: The first step toward getting somewhere is to decide you are not going to stay where you are. If you've ever seen a baby determined to move from one place to another to grab a toy or pet a dog or cat, you know that's true!

According to one site, 50 percent of babies have started walking by 12 months, but typically, a 12-month-old says only one or two recognizable words.[2] So apparently most of us learn to walk before we really talk. But in the Christian life, it's God's will that we do both at the same time. When people see our walk *with* him, it should make our talk *about* him believable. Therefore, we need to "walk the talk."

The purpose of our praying for wisdom to know God's will and the understanding to apply it is, then—as Paul wrote to the church in Colossae—so we "may live a life worthy of the Lord and please him in every way" (Colossians 1:10).

Now, the phrase "live a life" is just one word in the Greek language meaning "to walk," and in the Bible, the Christian life is often described as a walk. For example, read the following verses. One way or another, we're walking.

> If we claim to have fellowship with [the Lord] and yet walk in the darkness, we lie and do not live out the truth. But if we walk in the light, as he is in the light, we have fellowship with one another, and the blood of Jesus, his Son, purifies us from all sin (1 John 1:6-7).

> This is love: that we walk in obedience to his commands. As you have heard from the beginning, his command is that you walk in love (2 John 1:6).

When we walk to Jesus—taking our first step as a Christian—from that moment on we're to walk with him and walk for him. And this is to be a walk worthy of the Lord who walked to a cross for us. Jesus sacrificially died so that we would live for him, and the way he walked to the cross to his death is the way we should walk in life for him.

Dr. Casey Lewis wrote, "[Some Christians] can talk all about the Bible and 'churchy things' because they have been around it for most of their lives. However, when it comes to actually living according to the Bible's commands, they don't do it. They aren't then walking the walk. Instead they are just talking the talk."[3] Don't let that be you. We should please Jesus in every way.

H.P. Crowell, the founder of the Quaker Oats Company, lived by this statement: "If my life can always be lived so as to please Him in every way, I'll be supremely happy."[4] Every step we take should bring a smile to Jesus' face. Scripturally, belief and behavior always go together. What you really believe you live. The rest is just talk.

We must all ask ourselves these same questions every day:

- What steps will I take? Will they lead me closer to God or farther away?

- What path will I follow? The path of righteousness or the path of sinfulness?

- What actions will I take? Will they please someone other than God or please God even if they please no one else?

We're not here to please ourselves, so it doesn't really matter what we want. And we're not here to please the world, so it doesn't really matter what other people want. We're here to please the Lord, and so all that should matter to us is what he wants. Evangelist Lenard Ravenhill said, "If we displease God, does it matter whom we please? If we please Him, does it matter whom we displease?"[5]

I love the game of golf, but someone—possibly Mark Twain—described it as "a good walk spoiled." Daily and diligently, we must not allow the world, the flesh, or the devil to ruin a good walk. We must not fail to please God, doing our own will rather than his.

A young violinist giving his first recital did a magnificent job, but a man noticed that he always kept his eyes focused toward the second balcony. After the performance, he congratulated this young man and asked, "Why were you continually focused on the second balcony during your recital?"

The young man answered, "My master was up there, and from the smile on his face, I could see that he was well pleased. That's all that mattered to me."

Billy Graham wisely said, "There must be no discrepancy between what we say and what we do, between our walk and our talk."[6] Today, as opportunity arises, talk to others about God. But as you do, walk the talk!

Father, I witness both about you and for you in two ways—with my words and with my walk. May they always be in sync for your glory and pleasure. Amen.

WHERE'S THE FRUIT?

If my life is fruitless, it doesn't matter who praises me,
and if my life is fruitful, it doesn't matter who criticizes me.[1]

JOHN BUNYAN

Here are some interesting facts and the sad conclusion the pastor who shared them came to:

The bitternut tree does not bear fruit every year. It only bears fruit every three years and sometimes only every five years. The beech tree bears fruit every eight years. The white oak can go ten years without bearing fruit. But the champion in delay is the bamboo, which bears fruit only every 120 years! Few, if any of us, will live to be 120, but even if we did what a tragic 120 years it would be if we lived a fruitless life.[2]

As we continue to walk through Paul's prison prayer in Colossians, keep in mind that it's like a chain. One request is connected to the next—in sequence—so that one leads to the next. We know, then, that we should ask to know the will of God, through the wisdom of God, so that it produces a walk with God, all culminating in "bearing fruit in every good work" (Colossians 1:10).

As you can imagine, I've officiated at many funerals, and two kinds are particularly difficult for any pastor. One is the funeral of someone who never claimed to profess faith in Christ, who showed no interest in knowing him, and whose life even seemed to be devoid of any spiritual interest at all. But just as difficult is the funeral of someone who professed faith in Christ yet never exhibited any spiritual fruit.

Not only should we want Jesus to bear his fruit through us, but we should ask him to.

Of course, as mentioned in a previous devotion, we're not the root that bears fruit, Jesus. We're the branches. Andrew Murray wrote, "You are the branch...You need be nothing more. You need not for one single moment of the day take upon you the responsibility of the Vine."[3] Our job is to allow Jesus to bear his fruit through us.

Consider this illustration:

> The Associated Press released a study done by an agricultural school in Iowa. It reported that production of 100 bushels of corn from one acre of land, in addition to the many hours of the farmer's labor, required 4,000,000 lbs. of water, 6,800 lbs. of oxygen, 5,200 lbs. of carbon, 160 lbs. of nitrogen, 125 lbs. of potassium, 75 lbs. of yellow sulfur, and other elements too numerous to list. In addition to these things, which no man can produce, rain and sunshine at the right time are critical. It was estimated that only 5% of the produce of a farm can be attributed to the efforts of man.

The contributor of this illustration concludes, "If we were honest, we'd have to admit that the same is true in producing spiritual fruit."[4] In other words, the production of fruit through good works is the result of God's work, not ours.

And yet God chooses to bear fruit through us. We just have to prepare ourselves for this work. Any fruit-bearing tree or vine needs at least three things to bear fruit: to be rooted in good soil, the light of the sun, and the sustenance of fertilizer. The same is true for a fruit-bearing believer. We need our lives to be rooted in the soil of the Son of God. We need to be exposed daily to the light of the Word of God. And we need the sustenance of prayer in the Spirit of God.

In my decades of Christian life, I've found this to be true. When I'm daily planting my life in the soil of my relationship to the Son of God, exposing my life to the light of the Word of God, and then fertilizing my life in the Spirit of God, God naturally bears his fruit through me. And he will do the same through you.

I believe Jesus bears these types of fruit through us:

- *Christlike conduct*—This means we will act like Jesus. John 14:15 quotes Christ as saying, "If you love me, keep my commands." And in Galatians 2:20, Paul wrote, "The life I now live in the body, I live by faith in the Son of God."

- *Christlike character*—This means we will look like Jesus with "love, joy, peace, patience, forbearance, kindness, goodness, faithfulness" in our lives (Galatians 5:22). In 2 Corinthians 3:18, Paul says we are "transformed into his image."

- *Christlike converts*—This means that as his disciples did after Jesus commissioned them to do so (Matthew 28:19), we will lead others to Jesus. We will pray for those without Christ, talk to those without Christ, and ask the Holy Spirit to convict those without Christ to come to Christ.

Remember what Christ said about the importance of our remaining in him in order for fruit to appear:

> I am the vine; you are the branches. If you remain in me and I in you, you will bear much fruit; apart from me you can do nothing (John 15:5).

So ask yourself if you're allowing Christ to bear his fruit through you or if you're on the road to "nothing." For from John 15:16 we know Jesus said to his disciples, "I chose you and appointed you that you should go and bear fruit." That being true, ask yourself this hard question as you examine your life: "Where's the fruit?" knowing one prayer God will surely answer is to make sure you do.

God, I pray that you, the vine, will bear your fruit through me, the branch, in every good work I do—all to your glory. In Jesus' name, amen.

33

STAY ON THE GROWTH CURVE

The more we get to know God,
the more we want to know him better.[1]

D.A. CARSON

lbert Einstein is universally recognized as one of the most brilliant
men to ever live. He was a part of a pantheon of the greatest scientists
of all time, and it wouldn't be a stretch to say that today he would be
viewed as the GOAT (Greatest of All Time). They didn't measure IQ back in
his day, but it's estimated that his was at least 170.

Yet this intelligent and knowledgeable man made a statement about God
that is both revealing and heartbreaking:

> I once thought that if I could ask God one question, I would ask
> how the universe began, because once I knew that, all the rest is
> simply equations. But as I got older, I became less concerned with
> how the universe began. Rather, I would want to know why he

started the universe. For once I knew that answer, then I would know the purpose of my own life.[2]

How sad to contemplate that this brilliant man never understood what the purpose of his life was, which is the purpose of everyone's life: to know God. The God he wanted to question. The God to whom our purpose is to also bring glory.

In a previous devotion, I shared that out of all the books I've read, few have impacted me like *Knowing God*. In it, author J.I. Packer made this series of statements I want to repeat here: "What were we made for? To know God. To what aim should we set ourselves? To know God. What is the 'eternal life' that Jesus gives? Knowledge of God."[3]

Paul told the Colossians he prayed that they would be "growing in the knowledge of God" (Colossians 3:10). One commentator defines what having that knowledge means: "When we have knowledge of God, we understand his nature, his character, and who he is."[4] The only people who can truly pray to God, then, are the people who know God. And as they pray to the God they know, they are to pray that they will know him not just more but better.

Thousands of years ago, Moses lifted up a prayer we can offer now. He said to the Lord, "Teach me your ways so I may know you and continue to find favor with you" (Exodus 33:13). Moses knew he could grow in his knowledge of God and that his knowledge of God would please the Lord.

Here are three ways we come to know anything. Two of them won't help us in the way Paul means, but one will.

1. *Observation.* We can gain the simplest kind of knowledge this way. We know about something just by watching or looking at it. So, for example, we can look at the universe and know there must be a creator with incredible power. But we still won't know God.

2. *Education.* We come to know something by investigating, rationalizing, thinking, and studying. So we can read theology books, philosophy books, and religious books and learn a lot about God, but we still won't know God.

3. *Participation.* This is learning through personal experience. It's not just knowing about something or someone; it's truly knowing them by personal interaction and experience. This is the kind of knowledge of God Paul means here. We must have it and grow in it if we're to pray confidently and consistently. We must interact with our Lord every day through prayer and studying his Word.

Now, we can know God either casually or intimately, and here's the difference: If we know God casually, we know him by his works. We know what he can do. But when we know God intimately, we know his ways. We know him for who he really is. If we grow in our knowledge of him, we become more like him, we believe in him more, and we have assurance that we truly belong to him.

And there's a benefit to knowing God that we rarely think about. The better we know him, the better we know ourselves because the real us may not be the us we think we are. It's who God knows we are. John Calvin said, "Nearly all the wisdom we possess, that is to say, true and sound wisdom, consists of two parts: the knowledge of God and of ourselves."[5] In other words, growing in our knowledge of God, we will at the same time grow in the knowledge of ourselves. And the better we know ourselves, the more grounded we will be in who we are and who God wants us to be.

Consider this illustration: "After Mark Twain had made his triumphant tour through Europe, where he was honored by great universities and kings, his daughter said, 'Daddy, I guess pretty soon you will know everybody except

God.'"[6] Well, it's far better to know God and know no one else than to know everyone else but not know God. Thankfully, not only can we know the God who hears, but we can know him more—and better—every day.

One last insight from J.I. Packer: "How can we turn our knowledge about God into knowledge of God?...Turn each Truth that we learn about God into matter for meditation before God."[7] Stay on the growth curve!

Father, I know you through your Son, Jesus Christ, but may I never be satisfied with how much and how well I know you. May I know you better tomorrow than I did yesterday and know you today, and may my knowledge of you turn into praise and glory for you. Amen.

MORE POWER TO YOU

In whatever man does without God,
he must fail miserably—or succeed more miserably.[1]

GEORGE MACDONALD

A s I mentioned earlier, I've heard every objection in the book for why people refuse to surrender their lives to Jesus. Honestly, they're all just excuses because no valid objection to the gospel exists. A twentieth-century evangelist named Billy Sunday once defined an excuse as "the skin of a reason stuffed with a lie,"[2] and the majority of excuses I've heard fit that definition.

But one excuse isn't quite the lie the other excuses I've heard are, and it's the specific excuse I also mentioned earlier: "I could never live up to the Christian life." At least this excuse does express one truth. The people who say they can't live up to the Christian life can't—not on their own! And that's what I tell them.

That's not to say we might have doubts. Considering everything we've been saying about prayer, you might be thinking, *Do you realize what you're asking me to pray for? I'm not some super person. How on earth can I expect to do all these things, as good and holy as they are?* But think again. If you're a Christian, once you became a believer, how soon did it take you to realize you couldn't live up to the Christian life in your own strength and power, not even a little? Not long, right? The truth of the matter is not only can a person on their own not live the Christian life before they become a Christian, but on their own, they can't live the Christian life after they become a Christian!

Maybe what we all need is for the light to really come on: God never expected us to live the Christian life on our own. He never expected us to even try. Remember, in John 5:15, Jesus told his disciples, "Apart from me you can do nothing."

In his prison prayers—not once, not twice, but three times—Paul refers to the need to pray, asking God to strengthen us with his power. As a reminder, in Ephesians 1:19 Paul told the church he prayed for them to know God's "incomparably great power for us who believe." Then in Ephesians 3:16, he said, "May God strengthen you with power through his Spirit in your inner being." Now in Colossians 1:11, he says he prays for the church in Colossae to be "strengthened with all power according to [God's] glorious might."

I think when the Bible tells us something this many times, we ought to not just pay attention but really get serious about it.

Whatever God enlists us to do, he empowers us to do, and that power is available and at our disposal moment by moment. The Lord promises that he will give us all the power we need to do whatever he wants us to do whenever and wherever he wants us to do it. In 2 Peter 1:3 we read, "His divine power has given us everything we need for a godly life." God's power never gets overloaded and never shuts down, and the supply is inexhaustible. There's never a power shortage. And oh, by the way, you won't get a power bill because Jesus has already paid for you to have this power!

It's staggering to realize that we truly can be strengthened with all power according to the power of God! How often, like me, have you fallen into the

trap of trying to solve a huge problem with your own efforts rather than rely-
ing on the heavenly power within you? Maybe what we need to do is go out
at night and just look at the moon.

Consider this: If the moon were suddenly gone, the Earth's rotation would
eventually destabilize.

> Today, Earth's axis is tilted at 23.4° with respect to our orbit around
> the Sun. But there is a slight wobble in this spin cycle. The wobble
> is like the one you see with a spinning top, slowly making the tip
> trace a circle as the toy spins rapidly around. For the Earth, it's a
> rather slow wobble, taking around 26,000 years to go full circle.
> It's also quite gentle, moving the Earth's axis by just 2.4 degrees.
> But without the Moon to stabilize it, this wobble would become
> erratic and extreme.[3]

That seemingly small night-light keeps our planet stable. Jeremiah 32:17
says, "Ah, Sovereign LORD, you have made the heavens and the earth by your
great power and outstretched arm. Nothing is too hard for you." The God
we pray to created that moon with just a spoken word, but the power of the
moon amounts to a thimbleful compared to the ocean of the power of God
we swim in every day, often without even realizing it.

I don't know if you're facing a big problem or fighting a giant, but if you
are, you're only one prayer away from being strengthened with all power
according to the glorious might of the greatest power in the universe, your
heavenly Father. Alluding to the hardships he'd had to endure and yet found
contentment, Paul wrote to the Philippians, "I can do all this through him
who gives me strength" (Philippians 4:13).

Furthermore, never overestimate the problem, because you should never
underestimate the power you have at your disposal to face it. A little boy

was trying to move a heavy object, but it wouldn't budge, and he was nearly exhausted. His dad, who'd been watching the whole time, walked over to him and said, "Son, have you used all your strength?"

"Yes, sir."

"No, you haven't. You haven't asked for my help."

In the moment of your greatest weakness, remember that God's power is always available to you—and it's yours for the asking. Psalm 105:4 says, "Look to the LORD and his strength."

Father, I can't do what you want me to do and not even what I need to do in my own strength. When I face problems and giants, they're always far greater than my strength to handle them. Strengthen me with your power according to your glorious might, and by faith I accept that I have it, even now. In Jesus' name I pray, amen.

UNDER PRESSURE

A bend in the road is not the end of the road...
unless you fail to make the turn.[1]

HELEN KELLER

Are you under any pressure right now? If you are, I can empathize with you. Even as I'm writing these words, I've already missed one deadline for completing this manuscript, and I've got to make the next one or your opportunity to read this devotion will be greatly postponed.

In my years as a pastor, I've learned that when I talk to people about the issues they face, almost without exception I could lay the word "pressure" over what they're saying. Of course, at times, we all live under pressure. There's *family pressure*, like the pressure to find solutions when conflicts rise and tempers flare; *time pressure*, like the pressure to meet deadlines or get to appointments on time; *financial pressure*, like the pressure to ensure the money doesn't run out before the month does; and even *cultural pressure*, like the relentless pressure to conform.

God created the Mariana snailfish to withstand great pressure deep in the ocean, as outlined in a *National Geographic* article. "[These fish live] in total darkness and at crushing pressures that can reach 1,000 times more than at sea level" and "in a study published in *Nature Ecology & Evolution*, Chinese researchers examined the anatomy and genetics of the fish." The researchers found that:

- "The fish have gaps in their skulls…If the fish had a complete and fused skull, it would be crushed by the pressure."

- "Their bones are largely cartilage" and "this makes their bones more flexible and likely more able to withstand pressure."

- "The fish have high levels of a substance called trimethylamine N-oxide…which is used to stabilize proteins. Most animals have one copy…of [this] gene."[2]

There's more to know about these creatures, but the same wise, loving God who created them with the ability to handle such tremendous pressure in the ocean has given us what we need to handle the pressures we face. As we strive to love God, live for God, and stand for God—in society, culture, and a world increasingly moving away from God—we can, as Paul prayed, be "strengthened with all power according to his glorious might." And the result of that strength is "great endurance and patience" (Colossians 1:11). Endurance and patience are exactly what we need to deal with the two primary sources of pressure in our life.

The first is *difficult problems*. Often we have no choice but to endure the circumstances of a problem, or at least God calls us to endure them. The word "endure" means "to undergo especially without giving in."[3] In the military, the word refers to standing your ground in a battle. Let me remind you that life is not sailing down a calm river on a cruise ship. It's battling through rough seas on an aircraft carrier. But the one thing we can never do in life's battles is wave the white flag of surrender. What football coach Vince Lombardi said is true: "Winners never quit, and quitters never win."

I'm reminded of the power of endurance every time I visit Israel, where people speak Hebrew. It's the only nation in the world where it's the official language, largely because of one man:

> Hebrew had been a dead language for 2000 years. According to Nancy Bird, a professor of Hebrew language and literature at Washington University in St. Louis, its revival is unprecedented and unreplicated.[4] The reason why 9 million people speak this language today is because Ben Yehuda devoted his entire life to the restoration of the Hebrew language. For forty-one years he was ridiculed, called a fanatic, and shunned by many of his own friends who thought his effort was both futile and misguided. But because of this man's singular endurance, the Jewish people no longer speak 150 languages. They only speak Hebrew. And now, every Jew writes on their census form under "mother tongue," the word, *Hebrew*.[5]

The second primary source of pressure is *difficult people*. I personally believe it's easier to endure difficult problems than it is to deal with difficult people. I've seen more pastors leave the ministry because of challenging people than I have because of challenging problems.

Parents know the term "terrible twos," and I believe God created them just to teach us patience! Here's a principle I've found to be true: If someone gets the best of you (even a two-year-old), they bring out the worst in you.

A man was walking down the street with a two-year-old boy who wasn't having a good day. He was throwing temper tantrums, screaming, stomping, dragging his feet, and trying to pull away from his father at every turn. But the dad just kept calmly saying,

"Calm down, Albert."

"It will be all right, Albert."

"We'll get through this, Albert."

A woman standing off to the side saw all of this, walked up to the man, and said, "I admire the way you're handling this situation. It's encouraging to see how patient you've been with little Albert."

To her surprise, the man replied, "Oh, he's Sam. I'm Albert!"

When you're under pressure, turn to the God who hears, asking for his strength. Both the endurance and patience only he can give are available for the asking.

Lord, you know when I'm under pressure. You know the difficult problems I face and the difficult people I deal with. Give me the endurance and patience I need and can have as a follower of Jesus. In your Son's name, amen.

EVERY DAY IS THANKSGIVING DAY

O Lord that lends me life, lend me a heart replete with thankfulness.[1]

WILLIAM SHAKESPEARE

Toward the end of Paul's letter to the Colossians, he says he's prayed that they will give "joyful thanks to the Father" (Colossians 1:12). So let's take some time to consider a key component of any prayer—thanksgiving. And if you've read my book *How to Deal with How You Feel*, please forgive me for sharing several illustrations and thoughts—both in this devotion and the next—from that book. I just think they're too relevant to these topics to not revisit them.

Here's the story about the celebrated and highly successful author Rudyard Kipling:

> At the height of his popularity, a newspaper reporter approached him and said, "Mr. Kipling, I just read that somebody calculated that the money you make from your writings amounts to over $100 a word."

Mr. Kipling raised his eyebrows and said, "Really, I certainly wasn't aware of that."

The reporter cynically reached into his pocket and pulled out a $100 bill, gave it to Kipling and said, "Here's a $100 bill, Mr. Kipling. Now you give me one of your $100 words."

Kipling looked at the $100 bill for a moment, took it, folded it up, put it in his pocket, and then said, "Thanks."[2]

I also shared this thought in that book: "*Thanks* may have been a hundred-dollar word a century or two ago, but I would say today it's more like a million-dollar word. Today it's too rarely spoken, too rarely heard, and too often forgotten. It seems like we live in an ocean of ingratitude and walk in a desert of gratitude."[3] The attitude of gratitude should permeate not only our living but also our praying. Our heavenly Father should hear thanks from us every single day.

Note that Paul uses the word "giving." Thanksgiving is something we *give*. It's not something we necessarily *feel*. None of us always feels thankful, and feelings come and go. They're affected by the weather, the temperature, the functioning of our liver, how much rest we got the night before, or how the stock market is doing. Giving thanks has nothing to do with feelings, so we can give thanks even when we don't feel thankful. One might even argue that giving thanks is more meaningful when we're experiencing bad times than when we're experiencing good times.

I also shared these stories from Randy Alcorn and his concluding comment in my book *How to Deal with How You Feel*, and I really do think they bear repeating here:

In America, a sharp-looking businessman stands up at a luncheon to give his testimony: "Before I knew Christ, I had nothing. My business was in bankruptcy, my health was ruined, I'd lost the respect of the community, and I'd almost lost my family. Then I accepted Christ. He took me out of bankruptcy and now my business has tripled its profits. My blood pressure has dropped to normal, and I feel better than I've felt in years. Best of all, my wife and children have come back, and we're a family again. God is so good—praise the Lord!"

In China, a disheveled former university professor gives his testimony: "Before I met Christ, I had everything. I made a large salary, lived in a nice house, enjoyed good health, was highly respected for my credentials and profession, and had a good marriage and a beautiful son. Then I accepted Christ as my Savior and Lord. As a result, I lost my post at the university, lost my beautiful house and car, and spent five years in prison. Now I work for a subsistence wage at a factory. I live with pain from my neck, which was broken in prison. My wife rejected me because of my conversion. She took my son away and I haven't seen him for ten years. But God is good. He loves me, he has a plan for me, and I am so thankful.

Both men are sincere Christians. One gives thanks because of what he's gained. The other gives thanks in spite of what he's lost.[4]

Because God is sovereign and God is good, everything happening *to* you in his providence is also happening *for* you. That's why you can give thanks in every situation.

Here are some things to think about that might move your heart to break out into a song of thanksgiving. And, yes, these are also in my book *How to Deal with How You Feel*:

- If you woke up this morning with more health than illness, you are more blessed than the million who will not survive this week.

- If you have never experienced the danger of battle, the loneliness of imprisonment, the agony of torture, or the pangs of starvation, you are ahead of 500 million people around the world.

- If you attend a church meeting without fear of harassment, arrest, or torture of death, you are more blessed than almost three billion people in the world.

- If you have food in your refrigerator, clothes on your back, a roof over your head, and a place to sleep, you are richer than 75% of the world.

- If you have money in the bank, in your wallet, and spare change in a dish someplace, you are among the top 8% of the world's wealthy.

- If you can read this message, you are more blessed than over two billion people in the world that cannot read anything at all.[5]

When Abraham Lincoln was president, he started an unusual Thanksgiving tradition that every president since has followed. The Wednesday before Thanksgiving he pardoned the turkey. Following his tradition, the turkey is now brought into the Rose Garden, where the commander-in-chief grants that Big Bird a pardon. That turkey is then taken to a Virginia farm where he is granted immunity and lives out all of his days until a natural death. The only one in that event that doesn't give thanks is the turkey!

So as you pray, remember two things. First, don't be a turkey. Always pray giving thanks to your Father who gives you spiritual immunity from sin and eternal life forever. Second, no matter what the date is on the calendar, if you know Jesus, every day is Thanksgiving Day.

Father, thank you for the blessings of life and that you are always with me. No matter what comes my way, I know you will work it out for my good according to your purposes because I love you. In Jesus' name, amen.

37

BURSTING WITH JOY

Joy is the serious business of heaven.[1]

C.S. LEWIS

An old adage reminds us that it's not just what you say but how you say it that matters. And we can say the same thing about prayer: It's not just what you pray, but how you pray that matters. Through Paul's writing about his beautiful prayers, we learn about many things we should be praying for, uniquely not physical or material but spiritual. But then in Colossians 1:12, he shares *how* we should pray—"giving joyful thanks to the Father."

The Greek New Testament says, "*With joy* giving thanks." Joy and gratitude should go together, but they don't always, and it's possible to express gratitude without being joyful. A great example? If you've ever received a gift you didn't want or even hated, you might have put a smile on your face and said, "Thank you," but you certainly weren't joyful about it.

Paul is recommending that the Colossians always enter the presence of God in their prayer times with joy in their hearts. And as we've noted before, these prayers are also models for us. Note, Paul is not talking about happiness. Happiness and joy are not the same thing. In his book *Deadly Emotions*, Don

Colbert tells us happiness is a feeling of pleasure or well-being that comes from something outside of you. It's temporary. Joy is a feeling of pleasure and contentment on the inside of you.[2]

If your joy is in the Lord, it should be permanent. No matter what your circumstances may be, there should always be joy in your heart just from knowing you have the privilege of coming into the presence of your heavenly Father, that he will always give you his full attention, and that he always wants what's best for you.

That Greek word for "joy" is used 74 times in the New Testament, and it represents "a delight in the heart that is based on spiritual realities." One reason you should be full of joy when you pray—and why real prayer will make you full of joy—is that you're entering into the presence of the most joyful being in the universe. If you've entered God's presence, you've entered into heaven, and there is only joy in heaven.

Here's another story I told in *How to Deal with How You Feel*, this one about Joni Eareckson Tada, who became a quadriplegic, paralyzed from the shoulders down when she was injured diving into a lake at age 17. This comes from an article she wrote for *Decision* magazine:

> Honesty is always the best policy when you are surrounded by women in a restroom during a break at a Christian women's conference. One woman, putting on lipstick, said, "Oh, Joni, you always look so together, so happy in your wheelchair. I wish I had your joy!" Several women around her nodded. "How do you do it?" she asked as she capped her lipstick.
>
> "I don't do it," I said. "May I tell you honestly how I woke up this morning? This is an average day. After my husband, Ken, leaves for work at 6:00 a.m., I'm alone until I hear the front door open

at 7:00 a.m. That's when a friend arrives to get me up. While she makes coffee, I pray, 'Lord, my friend will soon give me a bath, get me dressed, set me up in my chair, brush my hair and teeth, and send me out the door. I don't have the strength to face this routine one more time. I have no resources. I don't have a smile to take into the day. May I have yours? God, I need you desperately.'"

"So what happens when your friend comes into the bedroom?" one of them asked.

I turn my head toward her and give her a smile sent straight from heaven. "It's not mine; it's God's." I point to my paralyzed legs. "Whatever joy you see today was hard won this morning."[3]

Well, joy is something you can both choose and choose to ask for. Either way, you will have it.

Joy is also a barometer of your relationship to God. If you're not full of joy right now as a child of God, and you're not full of joy when you pray, it isn't because you have a marital problem, a financial problem, an emotional problem, or a physical problem. You've got a spiritual problem. God is a God of joy, and when you're full of God, you'll be full of joy.

Here's one last illustration from *How to Deal with How You Feel*: "An article by an investigative reporter into what makes Disney World, Disney World, hit the bull's-eye with this statement: 'Every last brick that holds up Disney World is built to inspire joy for children.'[4] (If you ever go there and take kids or grandkids, you will not miss the joyful smile on the faces of those little ones.) The problem, as I said in that book, is that you can't take the joy of Disney World with you. When you leave, you leave the Disney joy behind. But the God of joy never leaves you. God goes with you everywhere you go, and so does his joy.

Whenever you pray, wherever you pray, and whatever you pray for when talking with the God who hears, do it with joy.

Father, help me remember that you are the God of everlasting, unending joy. I confess that I'm not always happy, but you never intended for me to be. Today in your presence, however, I choose to be joyful, and may others see the joy in my life that comes from knowing you. In Jesus' name, amen.

PERFECTLY QUALIFIED

*I know where my identity lies. My identity lies as a child of God,
and that is something that will never be shaken.*[1]

TIM TEBOW

Anytime we're considered for employment, two sets of criteria are probably at play. "Desirable criteria are skills and experiences that an employer would prefer, and essential criteria are the qualifications, experience, skills or knowledge you must have to apply for a role."[2]

What's true in the professional world is also true in the spiritual world. To be part of God's family, to have him as our Father and to be his child, we must be qualified. But here's the wonderful news: God does the qualifying.

God had a plan to qualify us through his Son and adopt us even when we were unworthy. Romans 5:8 says, "While we were still sinners, Christ died for us," making way for our inclusion in God's family. Though we were guilty as charged, Jesus wiped the slate clean, paid off our debt, got us out of the jail of sin, and set us free. But he didn't stop there to clear our name; he gave us *his* name. He didn't just get us out of jail; he took us home and gave us the title deed to his entire estate!

In his letter to the Colossians, Paul told the church he'd been praying that they would give thanks "to the Father, who has qualified you to share in the inheritance of his holy people" (Colossians 1:12).

Now, Colossae was in a Roman province, and Roman families—primarily wealthy families—adopted full-grown adults, mostly young men, not babies or children. They did this not only when their biological children had died but when they proved to be unworthy heirs. Men wanted a child they could trust to inherit their estate, so they would adopt a young man—rarely a young woman—and if he proved worthy, he'd be given the estate rather than any biological child in the family.

The concept of adoption would not, however, have resonated among the Jews, because adoption was not a custom for them. In Jewish terminology, there wasn't even a word for adoption. But Paul knew the people in Colossae were Gentiles by birth and living in a Roman province.

The Greek word translated into English as "adoption" (*huiothesia* [*uiJoqesiva*] "means to 'place as a son' and is used only by Paul in the New Testament."[3]

By Roman law, an adopted son

- lost all relationship to his old family and gained all rights to the new family,

- became heir to the father's estate,

- was forgiven of all prior debts, and

- was in the eyes of the law the son of his new father.[4]

Every single one of those things—loss of the old with a new right, inheritance, forgiveness, and a Father in heaven—is ours only because God has lovingly and perfectly qualified us. First John 3:1 says, "See what great love the Father has lavished on us, that we should be called children of God!"

If you've ever been part of an adoption, you know how wonderful this is, because adoption is always intentional. Nobody adopts because they have to; they adopt because they want to. I've heard of unplanned and unwanted pregnancies, but I've never heard of an unplanned or unwanted adoption.

I'm reminded of the siblings who constantly fought with each other. One day the brother popped off to the sister, "Well, you're adopted!" and the sister replied, "At least they wanted me!"

She had a point. As Todd Billings rightly noted, "The God of the Bible has no 'natural' or 'begotten' children apart from Jesus the Son; all the rest of us need to be adopted."[5] And the biblical truth is that everyone God calls his child was adopted into his family because he wanted them. Ephesians 1:5 says he adopted us "in accordance with his pleasure and will."

Because of our adoption, we have the right to call God our Father and ourselves his children, perfectly qualified to share in the inheritance of all of God's family in his kingdom. In fact, we are co-heirs with Jesus (Romans 8:17). John 1:12 says, "To all who did receive [Christ], to those who believed in his name, he gave the right to become children of God."

Mary Ann Bird was born with multiple physical defects, including deafness in one ear, and she endured the cruelty of children at school. One of the most difficult events for her was the annual hearing test, when a teacher whispered some short but meaningless phrase into the children's ears, such as "the sky is blue." If they were able to repeat the phrase back to the teacher, they passed. Fearful of failing, Mary Ann would cup her hand over her good ear so she could hear well enough to pass.

One year, Mary Ann was blessed to have a teacher named "Mrs. Leonard" who was the most beloved teacher in her school and was kind and gentle and this year Mary Ann would not have to cup her ear. Why? Because Mrs. Leonard didn't choose a random phrase like the "sky is blue" or "you have new shoes." As Mary Ann put it later, the teacher leaned across the desk, got as close as she could to Mary Ann's good ear and whispered, "I wish you were my little girl." Her life was at that moment completely transformed. She said, "I waited for those words which God must have put into her mouth, those seven words which changed my life."[6]

The Father constantly whispers one of two things in our ears: *I wish you were my child* or *I'm so glad you're my child*. Both speak of his love, but only the latter is possible for all who, through Jesus, are perfectly qualified. Henri Nouwen said, "Jesus came to announce to us that an identity based on success, popularity and power is a false identity—an illusion! Loudly and clearly he says, 'You are not what the world makes you; but you are children of God.'"[7] And because of God's grace and love we are perfectly qualified to say so.

God, I can call you Father and come to you as one of your children because you have qualified me to share in the inheritance of your family. Thank you for adopting me and making me what I am. In the name of your Son, amen.

THE GREATEST RESCUE

Christianity is a rescue religion.
It declares that God has taken the initiative in Jesus Christ
to rescue us from our sins.[1]

JOHN R.W. STOTT

For 17 days in June and July of 2018, the world was mesmerized by one of the greatest rescue efforts in history. A Thai junior association football team was trapped in the Tham Luang Nang Non cave in northern Thailand. Twelve members of the team, ages 11 to 16, and their 25-year-old assistant coach entered the cave on June 23 after a practice session.

Not long after, heavy rainfall began to partially flood the cave system, blocking their way out and trapping them in complete darkness two and a half miles from the entrance and 3,300 feet below the top of a mountain. The only route to reach them had several flooded sections, zero visibility, and complete darkness, and with some extremely narrow parts, the smallest measuring only 15 x 28 inches. Journeying through the cave to rescue these boys took six hours against the current and five hours to exit.

The rescue effort involved as many as 10,000 people, including more than

100 divers, scores of rescue workers, 900 police officers, and 2,000 soldiers. It required ten police helicopters, seven ambulances, more than 700 diving cylinders, and pumping more than 1 billion liters of water from the caves. But on July 10, the last four boys and their coach were rescued. Sadly, however, it came at the cost of two Navy SEALs' lives.[2]

This has been called one of the greatest rescue efforts in modern history, but in my opinion, it pales in comparison to the rescue described in the next part of Paul's Colossians 1 prayer: "[God] has rescued us from the dominion of darkness and brought us into the kingdom of the Son he loves" (verse 13).

We use several words or phrases for salvation, such as "redemption" and "the forgiveness of sins," which we'll see in the following devotion based on Colossians 1:14. But "rescued" is a word rarely used even though it's such an appropriate description of what's happened to every born-again believer.

If someone needs rescuing, they're helpless, just like those Thai young men were. And in so many cases, they're hopeless as well. Before we come to Jesus, we are all helpless, in a completely dark cave flooded with sin. And like those boys, we have neither the equipment, nor the expertise, nor the experience to get ourselves out. Indeed, our only hope is help from above.

The one thing those young men needed to survive was not education because they couldn't think their way out. And it wasn't money because they couldn't buy their way out. Not even oxygen tanks and diving masks would help because on their own, they couldn't swim their way out. The one thing they needed was a savior. They needed a rescuer, and so do we.

So many in the Bible needed and received God's rescue even before he came to earth for his greatest rescue. In the Old Testament we see

- Daniel, whom God rescued from a threatening lion attack, in their den because he'd prayed to the one true God.

- Rahab, whom God rescued from capture after she risked her life to save two spies from Israel.

- Shadrach, Meshach, and Abednego, whom God rescued when they were thrown into a furnace for refusing to bow down to King Nebuchadnezzar.

- Jonah, whom God rescued from the inside of a big fish, giving him another chance to do what God had asked him to do.

- The Israelites, whom God rescued over and over, from breaking their slavery in Egypt to delivering them from many troubles on the way to the promised land, including giving them protection from enemies.

But even if we never find ourselves in such dire situations, we were all born into what Paul called the dominion of darkness. We came into this world chained to sin, shackled by selfishness, serving the wrong god, going the wrong direction.

Someone described life without Jesus as a blind man in a dark room with no hope of finding the door to get out. But Jesus gave his life to not just take us out of that darkened room of sin but to bring us into the kingdom of light. Therefore we are to live as kingdom citizens here and now, knowing that one day we will live forever in the heavenly kingdom that is eternal. It's an indescribable privilege to not only be a kingdom citizen but a child of the King as well.

Charles Spurgeon rightly said,

> There is nothing for which the children of God ought more earnestly to contend than the dominion of their Master over all creation—the

kingship of God over all the works of his own hands—the throne of God, and his right to sit upon that throne…It is God upon his throne whom we trust.[3]

To become a naturalized citizen of the United Sates is a long process with at least ten steps. Not only do you have to be eligible, but you have to prepare and submit forms, pay fees, go to appointments and interviews, and wait for decisions and notices before you can take the official oath of allegiance to this country.[4] We have to admire immigrants who soldier through that lengthy and challenging process. And for some, citizenship is a rescue from a kind of darkness they fled.

But the moment we place our faith in the resurrected Lord, we become citizens of the kingdom of God. The God who hears has passed all the tests for us. He's paid all the fees for us. We have no interviews and no waiting. And he makes us kingdom citizens so we can show others that just as we were rescued from our sin, so can they.

Lord, thank you for rescuing me out of the dominion of darkness and bringing me into your kingdom of light. May the life I live and the words I speak be a tool in your hand to rescue others. In the name of the One who rescued me, amen.

DEBT-FREE

*Christ took the hell he didn't deserve so we could have
the heaven we don't deserve.*[1]

RANDY ALCORN

Being debt-free sounds like a dream come true to many American citizens, but debt is growing tremendously in this country. "American households carry a total of $17 trillion in debt as of the first quarter of 2023, and the average household debt is $101,915 as of the end of 2022."[2] The truth is that for too many people, debt-free seems like a pipe dream. For many reading this chapter, "debt-free" is not music to your ears. It's more like a bad tune you can't get out of your mind. Every morning you get up and go to work with a Disney-like lyric ringing in your ears: "I owe, I owe, so off to work I go!" Yet there's a kind of "debt-free" everyone can experience, a life that everyone can live, a blessing that everyone can have, and that is because of two gifts that Jesus gives to all who come to him.

Paul, I think, saved the best for last as we come to the final part of his prayer for the church in Colossae. He closes with reminding them that Jesus is the one "in whom we have redemption, the forgiveness of sins" (Colossians

1:14). When we receive Jesus, he gives us the two greatest gifts we could ever hope for—freedom and forgiveness. They offer a life everyone can live and a blessing everyone can have. God is the greatest giver in the world, and he will never allow his children to outgive him.

In the model prayer Jesus gave to the disciples, the one we call the Lord's Prayer, he expresses sin as debt: "Forgive us our debts," he says (Matthew 6:12). Because we are all born in sin, we are all born in debt. Sin puts us in debt to the God of the universe.

God is perfect, and because he's perfect, he rightly demands perfection from us. But it's a perfection we can never attain. We all sin daily, and so we pile up more sin debt day after day. Now, there's no way we can pay off the sin debt, but even if we could, we'd be back in debt before the day was over. That's because, frankly, when it comes to sin, we're all big spenders!

When you owe a debt you can't pay, only one thing can rescue you— redemption. When Jesus came to rescue us, he didn't just come to bail us out. He came to pay off our sin debt and free us from spiritual bondage once and for all. He came to redeem us.

Here's another way to look at this. First John 3:4 tells us sin is breaking God's law, and we're all law breakers. We accumulate a sin debt that must be paid. But only a perfect person who's never broken God's law and has no debt can get us out of debt, and that's exactly who Jesus is and what he did. While on earth, he perfectly kept the law. He never sinned in word, fault, or deed.

This is a mouthful, but don't gloss over it. On that day at Calvary, the Son of God didn't owe a debt he had to pay, and yet he paid a debt he didn't owe for a debt we owed and couldn't pay. He completely paid off our sin debt—forever.

Imagine that Satan has a ledger listing all the sins we've ever committed, and he decides to bring them to God to condemn us. But every time he opens the ledger to make his case, all the pages are totally blank except for one word stamped across each one—*redeemed!* No sin debt to collect. No sin payment to be made. Because of Jesus, we can look into the mirror every day and say these wonderful words: "I am debt-free!"

God not only gives us freedom but forgiveness. The debt hasn't just been paid off; it's been forgotten—permanently. It will never be brought up again.

Psalm 103:12, describing forgiveness, puts it beautifully: "As far as the east is from the west, so far has he removed our transgressions from us." And Max Lucado wrote,

> How far is the east from the west? Farther and farther by the moment. Travel west and you'll never go east. Journey toward the east and you'll never go west. Not so with the other two directions. If you travel north or south, you'll eventually reach the North or South Pole and change directions. But east and west have no turning points. Neither does God. His forgiveness is irreversible.[3]

Because of the God who hears, we are freely and finally forgiven!

I believe the Holy Spirit may have prompted Paul to write these last words because he was imprisoned when he wrote them. He wanted what every prisoner wants—freedom from prison and forgiveness for their crime (whatever the Roman authorities considered Paul's crime to be). And I think God had reminded him that he already had the most important freedom and forgiveness in his life—gained through Christ.

If you find yourself in a prison of problems so difficult and discouraging that it's hard to pray, think back on what we've learned on this journey and understand these three reasons you can pray—and with gratitude and praise:

- *Because of who and what you are.* You are a redeemed, forgiven person. Your debt has been paid, and your sinful record has been wiped permanently clean. You are forgiven, redeemed, and free.

- *Because of what you have.* You are God's child, and so he's positioned you to share in the inheritance of everything he has. He's qualified you to be one of his heirs, bequeathing you eternal life and unending fellowship.

- *Because of where you're going.* One day you'll go where there is no darkness, only light, and where there is no death, only life. Truly everyone in heaven lives happily ever after.

This is all true because you asked Jesus to live in you, and when he came, you gained direct access to all these gifts from the God who hears.

Father, I'm grateful beyond words that not only do you hear my prayers, but you assure me that they're always heard. Thank you for who and what I am, what I have, and where I'm going. May my prayers always be pleasing to your ears. In your Son's name, amen.

NOTES

INTRODUCTION: YES, GOD HEARS US

1. https: the blazingcenter.com/pray-quotes.
2. "54 Life-Changing Prayer Quotes—the Best of the Best!" the Blazing Center, https: The blazingcenter .com/pray-quotes.
3. Joseph Petro, *Standing Next to History* (New York: St. Martin's Press, 2005), 214-215.
4. "54 Life-Changing Prayer Quotes—the Best of the Best!" the Blazing Center.

CHAPTER 1: NEVER GIVE UP ON GOD

1. Marin Lyles, "Stay Motivated When the Going Gets Tough…" *Parade*, March 9, 2003, https://parade .com/980122/marynliles/not-giving-up-quotes/.
2. F.B. Meyer quote, Bible Reasons, https://biblereasons.com/prayer-quotes.
3. William McGill Quotes, AZ Quotes, https://www.azquotes.com/author/28958-William_J_McGill.
4. This comes from a personal email from Cas McCaslin.

CHAPTER 2: LOOK OUT AS YOU LOOK UP

1. Ananya Bhatt, "60 Praying for Others—Quotes to Bless Family & Friends," The Random Vibez, April 11, 2021, https://www.therandomvibez.com/praying-for-others-quotes/.
2. Janice Thompson Quotes: QuoteFancy, https://quotefancy.com/quote/666423/Janice-Thompson -May-those-who-love-us-love-us-And-for-those-who-don-t-love-us-May-God.
3. "41 Quotes about Intercession," Christian Quotes, https://www.christianquotes.info/quotes-by-topic/ quotes-about-intercession/.

CHAPTER 3: DO YOU KNOW WHO YOU ARE TALKING TO?

1. J.I. Packer, *Knowing God*, (Downers Grove, IL: InterVarsity Press, 1973), 29.
2. Story told by Dr. Howard Hendricks on March 4, 1982, at the International Congress on Biblical Inerrancy in San Diego, California. Cited by Kent Hughes, *Ephesians: The Mystery of the Body of Christ* (Wheaton, IL: Crossway Books, 1990), 57.
3. D.M. Lloyd-Jones, *God's Ultimate Purpose: An Exploration of Ephesians 1:1-23* (Grand Rapids, MI: Baker Book House, 1979), 344.
4. Doug McIntosh, *Holman Old Testament Commentary: Deuteronomy*, vol. 3, Max Anders ed. (Nashville: Broadman & Holman, 2002).
5. Lloyd-Jones, *God's Ultimate Purpose*, 329.
6. J.I. Packer, *Knowing God*, IVP Signature Edition (Downers Grove, IL: InterVarsity Press, 2021), 33.
7. James Montgomery Boice, *Ephesians: An Expositional Commentary* (Grand Rapids, MI.: Baker Books, 1997).

CHAPTER 4: OPEN THE EYES OF MY HEART, LORD

1. Helen Keller Quotes, AZ Quotes, https://www.azquotes.com/author/7843-Helen_Keller.
2. "The Wonders of the Eye, the Windows to Your Soul," Otay Ranch Eyeworks Optometry, https://orgeye works.com/the-wonders-of-the-eye-the-windows-to-your-soul/.
3. https://selecthealth.org/blog/2016/08/15-things-about-the-eye.
4. Paul Brand, MD, and Philip Yancey, *In His Image* (Grand Rapids, MI: Zondervan, 1987), 134-135.
5. Clara H. Scott, "Open My Eyes, That I May See," Hymnary.org, https://hymnary.org/text/open_my_eyes_that_i_may_see.

CHAPTER 5: THE GREATEST INHERITANCE

1. Nicky Gumbel Quotes, QuoteFancy, https://quotefancy.com/quote/1565413/Nicky-Gumbel-don-t-undervalue-yourself-God-loves-you-Your-worth-is-what-you-are-worth-to.
2. Mark Hall, "The Greatest Wealth Transfer in History: What's Happening and What Are the Implications," *Forbes*, November 11, 2019, https://www.forbes.com/sites/markhall/2019/11/11/the-greatest-wealth-transfer-in-history-whats-happening-and-what-are-the-implications/?sh=4749e0634090.
3. W.J. Seaton, "Philip and Matthew Henry," Banner of Truth, October 4, 2019, https://banneroftruth.org/us/resources/articles/2019/philip-and-matthew-henry/.
4. Harold W. Hoehner, *Ephesians* (Grand Rapids, MI: Baker Academic, 2002), 266.

CHAPTER 6: POWER UP

1. Wow4u, "50 Short Quotes about God," https://www.wow4u.com/50-short-quotes-about-god/.
2. Harold W. Hoehner, *Ephesians: An Exegetical Commentary* (Grand Rapids, MI: Baker Academic, 2002), 269.
3. "Megaton," *Merriam-Webster Collegiate Dictionary*, https://www.merriam-webster.com/dictionary/megaton#word-history.
4. Hoehner, *Ephesians*, 269.
5. Hoehner, *Ephesians*, 269.
6. Oswald Chambers quote, AZ Quotes, https://www.azquotes.com/quotes/topics/power-of-god.html?p=2.
7. Mark Batterson, *Primal: The Quest for the Lost Soul of Christianity* (Portland, OR: Multnomah, 2009), 152.

CHAPTER 7: STRONGER THAN YOU THINK

1. Kendra Tillman Quotes, Christian Quotes, Quoteschristian.com/strength/html.
2. Robert Kahn, "These Historic Strongmen…" History, updated June 24, 2019, https://www.history.com/news/strongest-men-in-history-most-famous-feats.
3. "Resurrection: What Are the Chances," It's Like This, http://www.itslikethis.org/resurrection-what-are-the-chances/.

CHAPTER 8: SIT NEXT TO ME

1. Charles Spurgeon Quotes, Prince of Preachers, May 30, 2017, https://www.princeofpreachers.org/quotes/sitting-at-the-feet-of-jesus.
2. Tim Keller, *Encounters with Jesus* (New York: Dutton, 2013), 173-174.
3. Keller, *Encounters with Jesus*, 176.

4. "Right hand," *Merriam-Webster Collegiate Dictionary*, https://www.merriam-webster.com/dictionary/right-hand.

5. Harold W. Hoehner, *Ephesians: An Exegetical Commentary* (Grand Rapids, MI: Baker Academic, 2002), 275.

6. Dr. Jerry Vines, "Our Ascended Lord," preached in Mobile, Alabama, at the Alabama Pastors' Conference in 1977 (Rome, GA: T.E.M, Inc., 1976), 36.

CHAPTER 9: THE ULTIMATE AUTHORITY

1. Ole Hallesby Quotes, Bible Portal, https://bibleportal.com/bible-quote/prayer-authority-prayer-is-the-risen-jesus-coming-in-with-his-resurrection-power-given-free-rein-in-our-lives-and-then-using.

2. Bob Buford, *Halftime: Moving from Success to Significance* (Grand Rapids, MI.: Zondervan, 2008), 150.

3. Buford, *Halftime*, 150.

4. Buford, *Halftime*, 150-151.

5. Charles Taylor, *A Secular Age* (Cambridge, MA: Harvard University Press, 2007).

6. Thomas Nagel, *The Last Word* (New York: Oxford University Press, 1997), 130.

7. Paul K. Mosher, "Divine Hiddenness, Death, and Meaning," *Philosophy of Religion: Classic and Contemporary Issues* (Oxford: Blackwell, 2008), 221-222.

8. Tim Stafford, *Surprised by Jesus* (Downers Grove, IL: InterVarsity Press, 2006), 207.

CHAPTER 10: IT'S HIS CHURCH

1. https://www.Christianquotes.info/quotes-by-topic/quotes-about-church/.

2. https://www.TheGospelCoalition.org/article/church-attendance/pandemic/.

3. Tim Keller, *Encounters with Jesus* (New York: Dutton, 2015), 4.

4. Ramsey Touchberry, "What Is the Waffle House Index? The True Story from the Man Who Created It, Craig Fugate," *Newsweek*, September 14, 2008, https://www.Newsweek.com/creig-fugate-explains-waffle-house-index-1120655.

CHAPTER 11: BEFORE YOU PRAY

1. Lauren Sanchez, "12 Inspiring Quotes about Prayer from Billy Graham," CrossWalk, February 26, 2018, https://www.CrossWalk.com/Faith/prayer/12-inspiring-quotes-about-prayer-from-Billy-Graham.html.

CHAPTER 12: POSTURE MATTERS

1. Victor Hugo Quotes, The Best Quotations, https://best-quotations.com/finder.php?gnom=Victor+Hugo.

2. John MacArthur, "Is There a Correct Posture for Prayer?" Grace to You, https://www.gty.org/library/Questions/QA156/Is-there-a-correct-posture-for-prayer.

CHAPTER 13: IN THE FAMILY

1. Mark Batterson and Parker Batterson, *If: Trading Your If Only Regrets for God's What If Possibilities* (Ada, MI: Baker Publishing House, 2016).

2. Deuteronomy 32:6; 1 Samuel 7:14; 1 Chronicles 17:13; 22:10; 28:6; Psalm 68:5; 89:26; Isaiah 63:16; 64:8; Jeremiah 3:4, 19; 31:9; Malachi 1:6; 2:1.

3. *Abba*, *Evangelical Dictionary of Biblical Theology*, ed. Walter A. Elwell (Grand Rapids, MI: Baker Books, 1996), 247.

4. Sarah Vallie, "What to Know about the Thoroughbred Horse," FETCH by WebMD, January 20, 2023, https://pets.webmd.com/what-to-know-about-the-thoroughbred-horse.

CHAPTER 14: POWER SURGE

1. "98 Quotes about Power," Christian Quotes, updated December 27, 2015, Christianquotes.info/quotes-by-topic/quotes-about-power/.
2. Adapted from John Stott, *Basic Christianity*, 50th Anniversary Edition. (Downers Grove, IL: InterVarsity Press, 2008), 123.
3. Major Ian Thomas, *The Indwelling Life of Christ: All of Him in All of Me* (New York: Crown Publishing Group, 2008).

CHAPTER 15: RIGHT AT HOME

1. R.W. Stott, *God's New Society: The Message of Ephesians* (Downers Grove, IL: InterVarsity Press, 1979), 135. Also compare Luke 24:18 and Hebrews 11:9.
2. John MacArthur, *The MacArthur New Testament Commentary: Ephesians* (Chicago: Moody Press, 1986), 106.
3. Steven J. Cole, "Making Christ at Home in Your Heart," Bible.org, https://bible.org/seriespage/lesson-22-making-christ-home-your-heart-ephesians-314-17a.
4. Francis Dixon, "Jesus at Home in the Heart," Words of Life Ministries, https://www.wordsoflife.co.uk/bible-studies/study-3-jesus-at-home-in-the-heart/.
5. Cole, "Making Christ at Home in Your Heart."

CHAPTER 16: FIRM AND DEEP

1. Paul Washer Quotes, Bible Reasons, https://biblereasons.com/gods-love-quotes/.
2. Tim Keller, *Preaching: Communicating Faith in an Age of Skepticism* (New York: Viking, 2015), 159.
3. Wes Seelinger, "Life in the Waiting Room," Preaching Today, https://www.preachingtoday.com/illustrations/1997/june/3236.html.

CHAPTER 17: UNLIMITED AND UNSURPASSED

1. Sabra Ciancanelli, "15 Amazing Quotes about God's Love," Guideposts, https://guideposts.org/daily-devotions/10-amazing-quotes-about-gods-love/.
2. Fritz Chery, "God's Love Quotes," Bible Reasons, May 22, 2013, https://biblereasons.com/gods-love-quotes/.
3. Fritz Chery, "God's Love Quotes."
4. "Story Behind the Love of God Hymn Lyrics," https://christianmusicandhymns.com/2022/07/story-behind-the-love-of-god-hymn-lyrics.html.

CHAPTER 18: IT'S BEYOND ME

1. Charlie Munger Quotes, WiseFamousQuotes.com, https://www.wisefamousquotes.com/quotes-about-knowing-what-you-dont-know/.
2. Mark Griffin, "How Fast Is Knowledge Doubling?" Lodestar Solutions, February 12, 2021, https://lodestarsolutions.com/keeping-up-with-the-surge-of-information-and-human-knowledge/.
3. Quote Investigator, https://quoteinvestigator.com/2018/11/18/know-trouble/.

4. Krista Carothers, "25 Facts You Learned in School That Are No Longer True," *Reader's Digest*, December 9, 2022, https://www.rd.com/list/facts-you-learned-no-longer-true/.

5. Chas. H. Gabriel, "My Savior's Love," Hymnary.org, https://hymnary.org/text/i_stand_amazed_in_the_presence.

6. Helen Keller quote, AZ Quotes, https://www.azquotes.com/quote/732684.

7. Anna Bartlett Warner, "Jesus Loves Me," Hymnary.org, https://hymnary.org/text/jesus_loves_me_this_i_know_for_the_bible.

CHAPTER 19: COMPLETELY FULL

1. "Full of oneself," *The Free Dictionary*, https://idioms.thefreedictionary.com/full+of+themselves#.

2. "Full of Yourself," Idioms Online, https://www.idioms.online/full-of-yourself/.

3. "What Is the Fullness of God (Ephesians 3:19)?": Got Questions? https://www.gotquestions.org/fullness-of-God.html.

4. "Free dive," *Merriam-Webster Collegiate Dictionary*, https://www.merriam-webster.com/dictionary/free-diving#:~:text=%3A%20to%20swim%20beneath%20the%20surface%20of%20water,two%20flippers%20%3A%20to%20engage%20in%20free%20diving.

5. "15 Freediving Facts You Need to Know…" Awesome Stuff 365, August 2, 2022, https://awesomestuff365.com/freediving-facts/.

CHAPTER 20: MORE THAN ABLE

1. Adrian Rogers Quotes, QuoteFancy, https://quotefancy.com/quote/1528151/Adrian-Rogers-Prayer-Can-Do-Anything-God-Can-Do-And-God-Can-Do-Anything.

2. "Doxology," *Merriam-Webster Collegiate Dictionary*, https://www.merriam-webster.com/dictionary/doxology.

3. James Montgomery Boice, *Ephesians* (Grand Rapids, MI.: Baker Books, 1997), 213.

4. Pamela Palmer, "34 Prayer Quotes to Uplift and Encourage Your Prayer life," Mother Teresa quote, Bible Study Tools, March 28, 2023, https://www.biblestudytools.com/bible-study/topical-studies/34-prayer-quotes-to-uplift-and-encourage-your-prayer-life.html.

CHAPTER 21: THE ENDGAME

1. Kyle Kizu, "How the MCU Built Up to Tony Stark's Final Avengers: Endgame Moment," Polygon, June 30, 2019, https://www.polygon.com/2019/6/30/18761619/tony-stark-death-avengers-endgame-quote.

2. "Endgame," *Merriam-Webster Collegiate Dictionary*, https://www.merriam-webster.com/dictionary/endgame.

3. Max Anders, "Why Does God Insist on Being Glorified?" https://www.maxanders.com/why-does-god-insist-on-being-.glorified/#.

4. "Glory," *Merriam-Webster Collegiate Dictionary*, https://www.merriam-webster.com/dictionary/glory.

5. "What does It Mean to Glorify God?" Got Questions? https://www.gotquestions.org/glorify-God.html.

6. Mark Batterson, *All In* (Grand Rapids, MI: Zondervan, 2013).

CHAPTER 22: GROWING UP

1. https://www.azquotes.com/quote /820532?ref=spiritual-maturity.

2. Kent Carlson and Mike Lueken, *Renovation of the Church* (Downers Grove, IL: IVP Books, 2013), 118-119.

3. Gregory Brown, "Marks of Spiritual Maturity," Bible.org, https://bible.org/seriespage/2-marks-spiritual-maturity.

4. I tweaked this illustration from Larry Crabb, *The Papa Prayer: The Prayer You've Never Prayed* (Nashville: Integrity Publishers, 2006), 40.

5. "What Is Spiritual Maturity?" Got Questions? https://www.gotquestions.org/spiritual-maturity.html.

6. Steve Farrar, *Tempered Steel* (Sisters, OR: Multnomah Publishers, 2002), 122.

CHAPTER 23: THE LOVE OF YOUR LIFE

1. Saint Augustine Quotes, AZ Quotes, https://www.azquotes.com/quote/12936?ref=love-grows.

2. C.S. Lewis, *Mere Christianity* (London: Fontana, 1952), 113-114.

CHAPTER 24: THE BEST CHOICE

1. Ryan Lilly Quotes, Goodreads, https://www.goodreads.com/quotes/tag/choosing.

2. Peter T. O'Brien, *The Epistle to the Philippians* (Grand Rapids, MI: Eerdmans Publishing Company, 1977), 77.

3. Alex Tresniowski, *Tiger Virtues: 18 Proven Principles for Winning at Golf and in Life* (Philadelphia: Running Press, 2005), 49.

4. Charles Swindoll Quotes, Brainy Quotes, https://www.brainyquotes.com/quote/charles_r_swindoll _457016?src=t_discernment.

CHAPTER 25: PASS WITH FLYING COLORS

1. Will Rogers Quotes, Goodreads, https://www.goodreads.com/quotes/9654-live-in-such-a-way-that -you-would-not-be.

2. A.T. Robertson, *Word Pictures in the New Testament* (Nashville: Broadman Press, 1931), 7.

3. Robert Hernan Cubillos, *Faith, Hope, and Love in the Kingdom of God* (Pickwick Publications, 2017), 343.

4. Jonathan Edwards Quotes, ForbesQuotes, https://www.forbes.com/quotes/5558/.

5. John Piper, "Will We Arrive Blameless on the Day of Christ?" Desiring God, March 10. 2012, https://www .desiringgod.org/articles/will-we-arrive-blameless-on-the-day-of-christ.

6. "With Flying Colours," Wikipedia, https://en.wikipedia.org/wiki/With_flying_colours.

CHAPTER 26: HIGH-HANGING FRUIT

1. https://www.Goodreads.com/quotes/1273084-don-t-shine-so-that-others-can-see-you-shine-so-that.

2. "What Is the Key to Bearing Fruit as a Christian?" Got Questions? https://www.gotquestions.org/bearing-fruit.html.

3. "What Is Righteousness?" Got Questions? https://www.gotquestions.org/righteousness.html.

4. Max Lucado, *Grace: More Than We Deserve, Greater Than We Imagine* (Nashville: Thomas Nelson, 2014), 23.

5. John Piper, "Bible Texts to Show God's Zeal for His Own Glory," Desiring God, November 24, 2007, https://www.desiringgod.org/articles/biblical-texts-to-show-gods-zeal-for-his-own-glory.

6. "20 Awesome Quotes about the Fruit of the Spirit," Christian Quotes, November 30, 2019, https://www .christianquotes.info/top-quotes/20-awesome-quotes-fruits-spirit/.

CHAPTER 27: NO WASTED TIME

1. Pamela Palmer, "34 Prayer Quotes to Uplift and Encourage Your Prayer life," Billy Graham quote, Bible Study Tools, March 28, 2023, https://www.biblestudytools.com/bible-study/topical-studies/34-prayer -quotes-to-uplift-and-encourage-your-prayer-life.html.

2. Charles R. Swindoll, *The Tale of the Tardy Oxcart* (Nashville: Word Publishing, 1980), 454-455.

CHAPTER 28: NO HARD STOPS

1. https://www.holycrosspdx.org/holy-cross-church/july-24-the-day-of-the-Lord-seventeeth-sunday-of-the-year/.
2. John Piper, "When Should I Stop Praying for Something?" Desiring God, August 22, 2014, Episode 413, https://www.desiringgod.org/interviews/when-should-i-stop-praying-for-something#Keep%20Askinglink.
3. Mark Batterson, *The Circle Maker* (Grand Rapids, MI: Zondervan, 2016), 35.
4. "Pepsi's New Super Bowl Commercial: Silence," CBS News, January 24, 2008, https://www.cbsnews.com/news/pepsis-new-super-bowl-commercial-silence/.
5. Jim Cymbala quote, Quote Sayings, "Quotes & Sayings About Persistent prayer," https://quotessayings.net/topics/persistent-prayer/.
6. Mark Altrogge, "12 Powerful Reasons to Persist in Prayer," The Blazing Center, https://theblazingcenter.com/2019/11/10-powerful-faith-building-reasons-why-we-should-persist-in-prayer.html.

CHAPTER 29: THE HYPHEN

1. Charles E Hummel Quotes, Bookroo, https://bookroo.com/quotes/charles-e-hummel.
2. John Piper, "What Is the Will of God and How Do We Know It?" Desiring God, August 22, 2004, https://www.desiringgod.org/messages/what-is-the-will-of-god-and-how-do-we-know-it.
3. Mark Batterson, *Draw the Circle* (Grand Rapids, MI: Zondervan, 2012), 224.
4. George W. Truett Quotes, Quote Fancy, https://quotefancy.com/george-w-truett-quotes.

CHAPTER 30: WHAT SHOULD YOU DO?

1. Adrian Rogers Quotes, Quote Fancy, https://quotefancy.com/quote/1528039/Adrian-Rogers-Knowledge-comes-from-looking-around-wisdom-comes-from-looking-up.
2. Lily Rothman, "Why It Is Easier Than Ever To Get Advice," October 22, 2015. https://Time.com/4082938/why-its-easier-than-ever-to-get-great-advice.
3. Mark Batterson, *Draw the Circle* (Grand Rapids, MI: Zondervan, 2012), 224.

CHAPTER 31: WALK THE TALK

1. "83 Notable Quotes by Dorothy Day…" The Famous People, ttps://quotes.thefamouspeople.com/dorothy-day-1255.php.
2. Sharon Perkins, "When Should Babies Start Crawling, Walking & Talking," Hello Motherhood, June 13, 2017, https://www.hellomotherhood.com/article/533794-when-should-babies-start-crawling-walking-talking/.
3. Dr. Casey Lewis, "Walk the Walk…" Christianity Matters, March 31, 2014, https://christianitymatters.com/2014/03/31/walk-the-walk-dont-talk-the-talk/.
4. Henry Parsons Crowell quote, The Christian Business Network, https://christianbusinessnetwork.com/resources/wisdom-at-work/entry/henry-parsons-crowell#.
5. Leonard Ravenhill Quotes, Goodreads, https://www.goodreads.com/quotes/747773-if-we-displease-god-does-it-matter-whom-we-please.
6. Billy Graham quotes, Christian Walk Quotes, https://www.wisefamousquotes.com/quotes-about-christian-walk/.

CHAPTER 32: WHERE'S THE FRUIT?

1. John Bunyan Quotes, Quote Fancy, https://quotefancy.com/quote/1113406/John-Bunyan-If-my-life-is-fruitless-it-doesn-t-matter-who-praises-me-and-if-my-life-is.

2. Robert C. Shannon, "Bearing Fruit," Preaching, https://www.preaching.com/sermon-illustrations/bearing-fruit/.

3. Andrew Murray Quotes, Goodreads, https://www.goodreads.com/work/quotes/265033-the-true-vine.

4. "Efforts of Man and Spiritual Fruit," Ministry127, https://ministry127.com/resources/illustration/efforts-of-man-and-spiritual-fruit.

CHAPTER 33: STAY ON THE GROWTH CURVE

1. D.A. Carson Quotes, AZ Quotes, https://www.azquotes.com/quote/1411967.

2. Jenish Modi, "Meaning of Life—Albert Einstein," July 9, 2021, https://goodqn.com/meaning-of-life-albert-einstein/.

3. J.I. Packer, *Knowing God*, IVP Signature Edition (Downers Grove, IL: InterVarsity Press, 2021), 33.

4. Clarence L. Haynes Jr., "How We Can Grow in the Understanding and Knowledge of God," Bible Study Tools, April 14, 2013, https://www.biblestudytools.com/bible-study/topical-studies/how-we-can-grow-in-the-knowledge-and-understanding-of-god.html#.

5. John Calvin, *Institutes of the Christian Religion*, ed. John T. McNeal, vol. 2 (Louisville, KY: Westminster, John Knox Press, 1960), 1.1.1.

6. "Twain's Knowledge of God," Preaching, https://www.preaching.com/sermon-illustrations/illustration-twains-knowledge-of-god/.

7. Knowing God Quotes, Goodreads, J.I. Packer quote, https://www.goodreads.com/work/quotes/276686-knowing-god.

CHAPTER 34: MORE POWER TO YOU

1. Warren W. Wiersbe, *Real Worship*, 2nd ed. (Ada, MI: Baker Books, 2000), 15.

2. Billy Sunday quote, CoolNsmart, https://www.coolnsmart.com/quote-and-anexcuse-is-a-skin-102511/.

3. "How Does the Moon Affect the Earth?" Institute of Physics, https://www.iop.org/explore-physics/moon/how-does-moon-affect-earth.

CHAPTER 35: UNDER PRESSURE

1. https://Identityglobal.com/my-top-10-perseverance-quotes/.

2. Douglas Main, "How the world's deepest fish survives bone-crushing pressure," *National Geographic*, April 15, 2019, https://www.nationalgeographic.com/animals/article/how-deep-sea-snailfish-survive-mariana-trench.

3. "Endure," Merriam-Webster Collegiate Dictionary, https://www.merriam-webster.com/dictionary/endure.

4. Earl Cornelius, "How the Hebrew language came back from the dead," *Lancaster Online*, March 30, 2019.

5. Albert St. John, *The Life Story of Ben Yahuda*, (Noble, OK: Balfour, 2013, Kindle locations, - 81,- 11113.

CHAPTER 36: EVERY DAY IS THANKSGIVING DAY

1. Katie Bowlby, "45 Short Thankful Quotes to Share Your Blessings This Year," *Country Living*, https://www.countryliving.com/life/g29536898/thankful-quotes/.

2. Mike Durbin, "A 100-dollar Word," *Baptist Beacon*, November 4, 2020, https://www.baptistbeacon.net/post/a-100-dollar-word.

3. James Merritt, *How to Deal with How You Feel* (Eugene, OR: Harvest House Publishers, 2022), 148.

4. Merritt, *How to Deal with How You Feel*, 150.

5. Merritt, *How to Deal with How You Feel*, 153.

CHAPTER 37: BURSTING WITH JOY

1. C.S. Lewis Quotes, Goodreads, https://www.goodreads.com/quotes/67336-joy-is-the-serious-business-of-heaven.

2. Don Colbert, *Deadly Emotions* (Nashville: Thomas Nelson Publisher, 2003).

3. James Merritt, *How to Deal with How You Feel* (Eugene, OR: Harvest House Publishers, 2022), 137-138.

4. Merritt, *How to Deal with How You Feel*, 136.

CHAPTER 38: PERFECTLY QUALIFIED

1. https://www.azquotes.com/quote/1591233? REF=child-of-God.

2. nhsbsa-live.powerappsportals.com/knowledgebase/article/KA-25715/en-us.

3. "Adoption," Bible Study Tools, https://www.biblestudytools.com/dictionary/adoption/#.

4. "The Spirit Confirms Our Adoption," Grace to You, May 29, 1983, http:www.gty.org/resources/sermons/45-59 /The-spirit-confirms-our--adoption?term = adoption.

5. Todd Billings, *Union with Christ: Reframing Theology and Ministry for the Church* (Grand Rapids: Baker Publishing Group, 2011), 18.

6. "On Compassion: The Whisper Test," Leader Helps, February 6, 2017 and 2017, https://leaderhelps.com/2017/02/06/On-compassion-the-whisper-test/ https://bolstablog.Wordpress.com/2012/2/16/whisper-test/

7. Henri Nouwen Quotes, AZ Quotes, https://www.azquotes.com/quotes/topics/child-of-god.html.

CHAPTER 39: THE GREATEST RESCUE

1. George P. Wood, "Basic Christianity," *Influence*, September 5, 2017, https://influencemagazine.com/en/Reviews/Basic-Christianity.

2. "Tham Luang cave rescue," https://en.wikipedia.org/wiki/Tham_Luang_cave_rescue.

3. "Divine Sovereignty," sermon by Charles H. Spurgeon, May 4, 1856, The Spurgeon Center, https://www.spurgeon.org/resource-library/sermons/divine-sovereignty/#flipbook/.

4. "10 Steps to Naturalization," U.S. Citizenship and Immigration Services, https://www.uscis.gov/citizenship/learn-about-citizenship/10-steps-to-naturalization.

CHAPTER 40: DEBT-FREE

1. Randy Alcorn Quotes, AZ Quotes, https:// www.azquotes.com/quote/1405018?ref = redemption.

2. Jack Caporal, "Average American Household Debt in 2023: Facts and Figures," The Ascent, May 17, 2023, https://www.fool.com/the-ascent/research/average-household-debt/.

3. Max Lucado, *Help Is Here* (Nashville: Thomas Nelson, 2022), 53-54.

OTHER HARVEST HOUSE
BOOKS BY JAMES MERRITT

9 Ways to Hold On When You Want to Give Up

52 Weeks with Jesus

52 Weeks with Jesus Devotional

52 Weeks Through the Bible

52 Weeks Through the Bible Devotional

52 Weeks Through the Psalms

52 Weeks Through the Psalms Devotional

Character Still Counts

God, I've Got a Question

The 25 Days of Christmas